Joan M. Edmunds was born in Worksop in Nottinghamshire. She was a member of the Theosophical Society for many years, but Joan's lifelong quest to discover the true significance of Joan of Arc's mission eventually led her to study the works of Rudolf Steiner. She joined the Anthroposophical Society in 1979 and for some years was editor of Rudolf Steiner Press in London. Now retired, she and her husband live in East Grinstead in West Sussex.

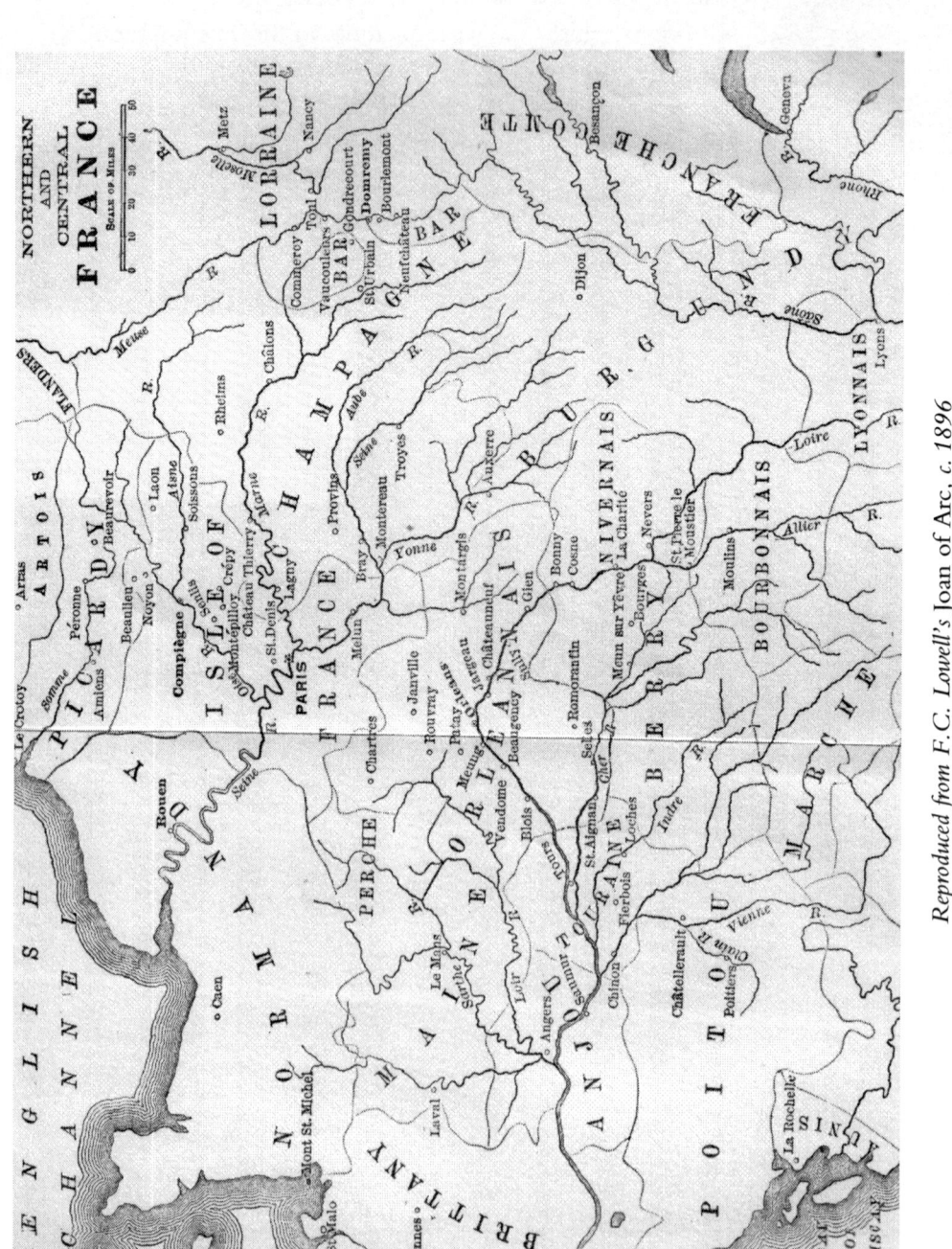

Reproduced from F.C. Lowell's Joan of Arc, c. 1896

THE MISSION OF JOAN OF ARC

Joan M. Edmunds

TEMPLE LODGE

Temple Lodge Publishing
Hillside House, The Square
Forest Row, RH18 5ES

www.templelodge.com

Published by Temple Lodge 2008

© Joan M. Edmunds 2008

The moral right of the author has been asserted under the Copyright, Designs and Patents Act, 1988

All rights reserved. No part of this publication may be reproduced, stored in a retrieval system, or transmitted, in any form or by any means, electronic, mechanical, photocopying or otherwise, without the prior permission of the publishers

A catalogue record for this book is available from the British Library

ISBN 978 1 902636 97 9

Cover by Andrew Morgan incorporating an image of a head of a statue reputed to be of Joan of Arc
Typeset by DP Photosetting, Neath, West Glamorgan
Printed and bound by Cromwell Press Limited, Trowbridge, Wiltshire

Contents

Preface		1
Introduction		8
1	Domremy	12
2	Vaucouleurs	23
3	Chinon	30
4	Orléans	43
5	The Loire Campaign	57
6	Reims	65
7	Towards Paris	71
8	Victory—and Defeat	78
9	Capture	83
10	The Final Journey	91
11	Imprisonment	99
12	The Trial: Part One	105
13	The Trial: Part Two	126
14	Abjuration and Relapse	133
15	Martyrdom	139
16	Rehabilitation	148
Afterword		162
Principal Sources		165
Bibliography		168

*To my dear husband,
Kenneth Thompson,
for his loving support
during the writing of this book*

   ...Yet I am well content
To think that I have passed in such employ
The green and vigorous season of my mind,
And hope that there are those in whom the song
Has woke some not unprofitable thoughts.

Robert Southey

Preface

In his lecture cycle *Occult History*, Rudolf Steiner draws our attention to what he calls 'a very common practice in our so-called civilization'—and this, he says, is 'to wish to correct the deeds of gods through human intellect'.

The deed of the gods to which he is specifically referring is that which was expressed through the life and mission of one of the greatest personalities, one of the most unique incarnations of western history—that of Jeanne d'Arc—Joan of Arc, as she is more widely known to English-speaking people. Also known as the Maid of Orléans, Maid of France, or simply as 'the Maid', Joan spoke of herself as 'Daughter of God' and Rudolf Steiner said that the mission of Joan of Arc in the fifteenth century *was* a deed of the gods, a deed against which were ranged the most powerful adversaries, working in an attempt to hinder, even destroy, the great task she had to accomplish.

In our time there are also adversaries at work against her, and they are those to whom Rudolf Steiner refers—they are certain modern biographers of Joan of Arc who, by the solely intellectual approach to her life seek, as he says, 'to unburden history of her deeds'. In the time that has passed since Rudolf Steiner accused Anatole France of being 'an entirely obsessed materialist' in interpreting the *facts* of her life in such a sceptical and ironic manner, further often quite bizarre attitudes have developed, such as attributing her inspirations to a variety of physical and psychological disorders—in fact, in ways feasible to the human mind as it is influenced by modern materialistic and scientific thought.

Of the thousands of books and studies written about Joan of Arc since the nineteenth century (she is the third most documented historical figure, the others being Christ and Napoleon), there are many excellent works by reputable historians and by eminent biographers dealing with the facts of her life taken from the large number of legal documents and records which have survived in the archives in France since the fifteenth century. But there are equally as many works whose authors have attempted to *explain* her life and actions, which are of such a nature as to amount to a total denial of those Spiritual Powers that worked in a necessary and significant way at the beginning of our epoch. By grossly distorting the historical facts or by simply ignoring them, the reader is presented with something that is more 'understandable', with 'revelations' with which their authors have 'solved' the mystery of her life.

And so today, almost six centuries after her death, the life of Joan of Arc still exerts a strong fascination, but to those who read about her she remains an enigma—and to many, simply a fraud.

It is indeed virtually impossible for the modern mind to accept that, in the early part of the fifteenth century, a young peasant girl, only twelve years of age, entered into communion with a mighty Spiritual Being, and was instructed by him and, later, by other spiritual entities, and also by discarnate human beings in the spiritual world, in preparation for a great task. This communion continued throughout the seven years of life which remained to her, until her death at the age of 19—a martyr's death at the stake.

The true nature of the enormous task accomplished by Joan of Arc must always remain beyond the comprehension of the world at large, unless there is a willingness to strive for a deeper understanding of an event which was of the greatest significance for future human development.

Regarding the usual interpretations of history, upon which people make their judgements, Rudolf Steiner has said that, as with the life of feeling, mankind dreams away the true impulses of history, because people write history with the same thoughts and concepts they employ in external, ordinary life; and because there is no real knowledge that the historical life of mankind is governed by impulses which cannot be grasped with the concepts of our waking consciousness, the only way to understand what works in history is with inspired concepts, with inspiration—which, he further elucidates, is by way of clairvoyant consciousness.

Joan of Arc herself spoke in a similar vein concerning the enigma of her life and mission when, to those around her, who marvelled at her actions, she spoke about the mystery of her achievements. When her chaplain, Jean Pasquerel, said to her, 'Such things have never been seen, as have been seen in your deeds; in no books are comparable feats to be read,' Joan replied, 'My Lord has a book in which no clerk has ever read, however learned he may be.' She also hinted about this to the corrupt Catholic churchmen, with whom she battled so bravely during her trial, and warned them about passing judgment on what they did not understand.

Almost five centuries after Joan's death, understanding by the Catholic Church had still only progressed to the extent that, by 1920, although finally placing her on its Calendar of Saints, it had failed to recognize her true significance, and canonized her simply as 'Virgin'.

But what of Joan's enigmatic statement regarding the 'book', the 'book of my Lord', in which no clerk, i.e., cleric or scholar, had ever read—signifying that only there would the truth about her actions be found? Biographers have noted her words, but have never ventured an explanation.

All Joan's words and deeds were inspired by, and taught to her by what she called her 'Heavenly Counsel', or her 'Voices'; she was innocent and unlearned and accepted their instructions without question. From her own words we know that secrets of a deeply esoteric nature were revealed to her—as she said, 'shown' to her—although she may not always have fully understood their meaning. Among those secrets, however, we may infer that the nature of the 'book' was, to some extent, also revealed to her.

Throughout the centuries, Joan's enigmatic words about the 'book' have remained a mystery; ignored by biographers or, perhaps, regarded by them as incapable of intelligible explanation. However, what has been revealed by modern research into the nature of the spiritual worlds, by Rudolf Steiner and other investigators, has now made it possible to identify the 'book', with which Joan so defiantly challenged her judges, as the Akashic Record—that indelible imprint in the astral light, in which all the past events of the world are displayed.

★ ★ ★

Rudolf Steiner has given us great insight into tremendous events taking place in both the physical and the spiritual worlds at the beginning of the fifteenth century. Of the former, he says:

Let us picture to ourselves that in the 15th century, England had been diverted from its desire towards that part of the earth which was opened up through the discovery of the great continents beyond Europe, and that the British Folk-Soul had then undertaken significant extensions of territory on the continent of Europe. In the first place it would then have been impossible to attain that material culture which had to be attained, and secondly, Europe would not have attained that deepening of its inner life which, notwithstanding many hindrances, developed from that time through the co-operation of Protestantism greatly influenced by German mysticism. The Christ Impulse having intervened in evolution, it had to take care to keep British interests far from the domain in which souls had to be prepared to be the external bearers of the Christ Principle.

This period was the dawn of the 5th post-Atlantean epoch of civilization, when Central Europe would enter the age of the Consciousness or Spiritual Soul. As we know, the age began in the year 1413, and its characteristic is that which is able to develop by turning its attention to the material life and to the external facts of physical existence. The British Folk-Soul is especially chosen for the unfolding and development of the Consciousness Soul—this was absolutely pre-arranged in the plans for the development of mankind.

Of events in the spiritual world:

As one looked down to the earth, one witnessed, as it were, how Seraphim, Cherubim and Thrones—the members of the highest Hierarchies—were accomplishing a mighty deed ... an awe-inspiring departure from what is thus seen in the ordinary course of being. It was in the Atlantean time that such a thing had last shown itself, as seen from the aspect of the supersensible ... when the Cosmic Intelligence, while remaining cosmic, had taken possession of the hearts of men ... and now for the present earthly realm it once again broke forth in spiritual lightning and thunder. In the age when men were conscious of the earthly historic convulsions only ... when all manner of remarkable events were happening of which you can read in external history—in that age the earth appeared, to the spirits in the supersensible worlds, surrounded by mighty lightnings and thunderclaps. The Seraphim, Cherubim and Thrones were carrying over the Cosmic Intelligence into that member of man's organization which we call the system of nerves and senses, the head-organization. Once again a great event had taken place. It does not show itself distinctly as yet, it will only do so in the course of hundreds or thousands of years; but it means ... that man is being utterly transformed. Formerly he was a heart-man; then he became a head-man. The Intelligence becomes his own.

★   ★   ★

From ancient times the Archangel Michael had guarded the Cosmic Intelligence in the cosmos, but since it had descended to the earth it had become human intelligence.

Of the seven successive cyclic rulerships of the archangelic Beings who guide the evolution of humanity, Samael was at this time the Leading Spirit. Michael would not assume his dominion again until the end of the nineteenth century. But now, working in the spiritual world, a great and significant event took place, when Michael assumed leadership of what Rudolf Steiner calls 'a supersensible School'. In this assembly, Michael gathered around him those spiritual Beings who never incarnate on earth but are connected with the evolution of humanity, and those of his stream who were in the life between death and rebirth, that is to say, those members of humanity who had worked for and with him through many ages upon the earth.

Michael now began to teach those around him about a great task in the future, when an intelligence bereft of spirituality would gradually take root among men; a crisis would develop from the fifteenth century onwards, with the ahrimanic powers growing ever stronger in their efforts to keep the intelligence totally earthly. The call to those around Michael was to work towards the time when, in the latter part of the nineteenth century, Michael would once again assume his role of the guiding Spirit, in order that the intelligence might once again be united with his Being.

★   ★   ★

It was against this background of mighty cosmic events that Joan of Arc was born—in the year 1412, the year preceding that which saw the birth of the Spiritual or Consciousness Soul. Rudolf Steiner speaks of the mystery surrounding her birth:

> If the soul does not consciously seek initiation as delineated in *Knowledge of the Higher Worlds: How is it Achieved?*, but becomes saturated with the Christ Impulse as if by way of natural initiation, then the most favourable period for this process is from 25 December to 6 January ... During the last few days prior to a person's birth he lives in the mother's womb in a dreaming, sleeplike state. He has not yet perceived with his senses what is happening in the world outside. If by virtue of his karma a person were especially suited to receive the Christ Impulse during these last few days in the womb, then these days could also be days of natural initiation. Strengthened by and saturated with the Christ Impulse, such a person would have to be born on the sixth day of January. Joan of Arc was born on that day. It is her special mystery that she was born on the sixth day of January and had spent the time from Christmas to the day of Epiphany in a peculiar sleeplike state in the womb of her mother where she received her natural initiation. Now consider the profound connections beyond the external developments that we are accustomed to call history. As a rule, the external events that are reconstructed from historical documents are of the least significance. What is of decisive historical significance is the plain date in our calendar indicating that Joan of Arc was sent into the world on the sixth day of January. Thus, supernatural forces become active in the sentient world and we must read the occult signs that present this fact to us. They tell us that the Christ Impulse had already streamed into the Maid of Orléans before her physical birth, as if by way of natural initiation.

Rudolf Steiner has further explained that, in this time before Joan's birth, it was the Archangel Michael who had deeply impressed her mission upon her soul and astral body; and it was at the time of the birth of the astral body in human life, in Joan's case from the age of twelve, that she first experienced her clairvoyant and clairaudient awakening to the presence of Michael.

In considering this time of year in which Joan was born, we know that there are two periods in the cycle of the year when the earth is, in a sense, wholly united with the heavens—'when the soul of the earth holds its breath', as Emil Bock has aptly expressed it. In the Holy Nights, when the earth has breathed in its utmost, when it is in its most spiritual state—this time saw the birth of Joan into the physical world; it was also the time of year from which her mission would begin.

In direct contrast to the Holy Nights, in midsummer, St John's tide, when the earth breathes out and its soul passes out to the heavens—this was the time when Joan would experience a second 'birth': that of her conscious, spiritual awakening.

Introduction

Until the beginning of the nineteenth century, the authentic historical details of the life of Joan of Arc were little known; although her name had been kept alive throughout the centuries, it had become interwoven with legend and myth. Historians and other writers of earlier times had commented on her according to their nationalistic sympathies—Shakespeare is an example of this approach. Others, such as Schiller and Southey, had a rare insight into her real nature, even though they were unaware of many of the historical facts.

It was at the beginning of the 1840s, at a time when, as Rudolf Steiner tells us, great battles were being fought in the spiritual world bordering on the physical world, that Joan of Arc reappears with great clarity before the consciousness of Europe—the servant of Michael comes, in a sense, into the world-view at a time when the Archangel Michael is engaged in another conflict with those Powers which are his adversaries.

It is of real significance that the historical facts of the life of Joan of Arc should come to light at this particular period, and that the truth should gradually become known about the one who was the herald of the age in which we are living today. There was a great upsurge of interest in her life in the nineteenth century, the tide of which flowed on into the twentieth, culminating in her canonization in 1920.

In 1841, the eminent French scholar, Jules Quicherat, collected and translated some of the great mass of surviving historical documentation on Joan for the Société de l'Histoire de France. His work was compiled from the official Latinized report of the trial known as the Authentic Document, which, although still of value today, has been considerably extended by later Johannic scholars from documents in various French archives. For general purposes, this great mass of evidence may simply be referred to as, firstly, the proceedings known as the Trial of Condemnation, which led to Joan's death, and the later inquiry instigated by Charles VII, which completely exonerated her of all the false claims made against her at the first trial, known as the Trial of Rehabilitation. Both trials give an absolutely vivid picture of Joan's life and mission, both in her own words and those of her contemporaries—the villagers who knew her from birth, her friends and companions, members of the noble houses of France, the knights who fought at her side, her enemies, and the clergy, both sympathetic and hostile. All of these speak clearly of the great drama that was the life of Joan of Arc. Not only do we possess these extraordinarily detailed testimonies, but there is also the unique fact that her life is the only one to come down to us in history, sworn on oath in a court of law.

Of the many excellent English and French writers on Joan of Arc and her mission, a large number of these works are, unfortunately, now out of print or unavailable in English translation. Two of the most accessible writers, both eminent Johannic scholars and totally dependable authorities for the external historical facts, are the English writer—a very dear friend of this author—the late Revd Dr W. S. Scott, and the admirable French historian and medieval scholar Régine Pernoud, a number of whose works are available in translation.

But it is from the great spiritual insight possessed by Rudolf Steiner, that we are able to learn about the previously hidden truths and discover the real meaning of the life and mission of Joan of Arc. With his guidance we can approach her life with that reverence which, he tells us, we must have for such personalities, if we are to understand the working of the spiritual in the physical world.

Between the years 1911 and 1924, Rudolf Steiner spoke on a number of occasions about Joan, most notably at the start of the First World War in 1914 and again in 1915, when he described in vivid and decisive detail the significance of her life and mission for European evolution and for the emergence of the Spiritual or Consciousness Soul. His words leave us in no doubt that we are, at last, in possession of the true interpretation of an event without parallel in the history of western civilization.

Concerning crucial stages in European history, Rudolf Steiner spoke of two events which have influenced the development of the entire western world. The first of these was the triumph of Constantine the Great who, by his success at the battle with Maxentius in AD 312, was able to introduce Christianity into the external religious life of Europe.

The second decisive event occurred during the long struggle

between England and France in the fourteenth to fifteenth centuries, which became known as the Hundred Years' War. This was basically a dynastic quarrel between the royal houses of the two countries. Additionally, France was not yet a united kingdom, but in claiming the Armagnac right to the throne Charles VI of France was not only at war with England, but was continually embroiled in clashes with his rival for power and ally of England, Philippe the Good, the Duke of Burgundy.

Following France's crushing defeat at Agincourt by Henry V in 1415, and later English victories, the fortunes of France were at their lowest ebb. The prolonged horror and devastation caused by the wars was bringing the country almost to the point of total collapse and ruin.

In 1420, Henry V laid claim to his right to the throne of France, and an attempt was made to end the strife between the two kingdoms with the signing of the Treaty of Troyes, which took place in May of that year. Under the terms of the Treaty, the ailing king had been persuaded by his wife, the infamous Isabeau de Bavière, to insert a clause disinheriting his only surviving son, the Dauphin Charles, which in effect declared him a bastard and therefore not his rightful heir—a situation regarded by some as a distinct possibility, in view of Isabeau's many notorious affairs. This ruthless and dissolute queen had more or less held the reins of the country for many years because of the king's frequent bouts of madness—she would become even more notorious after the appearance of Joan of Arc, when she would become the focus of a famous prophecy.

The Treaty of Troyes had recognized Henry as heir apparent to the French throne; the alliance was further strengthened by Henry's marriage to Charles' daughter, the Princess Catherine. But in 1422 the situation in both countries changed dramatically when Henry V died, leaving an infant son by Catherine. Charles VI died two months later, leaving his only son, the Dauphin Charles, in a precarious situation because of Isabeau's denial of his legitimacy.

The 'so-called Dauphin', as he had been designated in the Treaty, declared himself Regent of France, but his own nature and the circumstances in which he found himself left him unable to take any action to secure his throne. A weak and indolent youth of 19, he was unfortunate in every respect, not least in his physical appearance. He had a long, dour face, small, grey shifty eyes, a bulbous nose and pendulous lip. His body was also ill-formed and ungainly—a contemporary chronicler would later describe him as 'the ugliest man in Christendom'.

He had a bitter enemy in Philippe, the powerful Duke of Burgundy, whose father, Jean sans Peur (the Fearless), had been assassinated at Montereau in 1419, in a vendetta by the Armagnacs to avenge the murder of Duke Louis of Orléans in 1407. Charles had been present at the murder scene, although it is not known whether he was actually involved in the plot. Philippe afterwards publicly declared that his father's assassin should never take the throne of France. In pursuit of this revenge he received the support of Isabeau de Bavière, which led directly to the Treaty of Troyes.

Bereft on all sides, the hapless Dauphin eventually took refuge from his enemies in the largely Armagnac controlled south, living between various châteaux in the Loire region. Here he was surrounded by an assortment of unscrupulous courtiers and so-called advisers, amongst whom was the treacherous Georges de la Trémoille, from whom the impoverished Charles borrowed money to maintain his shabby court. Presumably these men stayed with him in the slender hope that they would benefit, should he one day claim his throne.

By 1424, the state of both countries was still totally unresolved. Henry V's brother, John of Lancaster, Duke of Bedford, was guardian of the infant Henry VI, and had been appointed Regent of France and Governor of Normandy, Paris and the north, territories earlier wrested from the French. At this time and in the years ahead, treaties, negotiations and truces would continue between the Armagnacs and the Anglo-Burgundians, but without any lasting peace or resolution of France's chaotic situation.

★ ★ ★

Far away from the turmoil, in a small village in north-eastern France, a young girl, only twelve years of age, who was to resolve the destinies of the two nations, experienced for the first time the presence of a mighty Spiritual Being who, from an initial, gentle guidance over the ensuing years, would gradually reveal to her, with ever-increasing intensity, the great destiny she must fulfil.

1   Domremy

Joan of Arc was born in the village of Domremy, later to be called Domremy-la-Pucelle in her honour—*pucelle* being the old French word for 'maid'. The village is situated in the valley of the Meuse in north-eastern France. In Joan's day, it was in an unusual geographical position, standing on the frontier between what was, at that time, France, Burgundy and the Duchy of Bar. Today it is on the western borders of Lorraine, six miles north of the town of Neufchâteau and twelve miles south-east of Vaucouleurs.

Joan was the fourth of the five children of Jacques and Isabelle d'Arc. Her three brothers were Jacques, Jean and Pierre. Catherine, born after Joan, is believed to have died some time during the latter part of Joan's mission.

The parents had a good reputation in the community, and Joan's father was *doyen*, or head-man of the village. In the testimony taken from the villagers for the Rehabilitation proceedings they were in accord that Jacques and Isabelle were devout Catholics and greatly respected by everyone.

Little more is known about Jacques d'Arc, but there is one significant incident, which came to light at Joan's trial, when her judges were questioning her closely about her life before she left home:

> What was the dream your father had about you before you left his house?
>
>   I was several times told by my mother that my father had told her that he had dreamt that I would go away with soldiers. My mother and father were greatly concerned and they watched me closely and kept me in great subjection.

One can imagine that Jacques' dream would be the cause of great upheavals in the d'Arc household as, naturally, he feared the worst; girls who followed armies were usually little more than prostitutes, and this bluff peasant farmer must have exploded with anger at his distressing dream. Joan told her judges:

I have heard my mother say that my father told my brothers that if this should happen, 'I would rather you drowned her, and if you would not do it, I would drown her myself.'

Although Joan said that she always obeyed her parents, she obviously remained silent as to the true nature of her impending departure. Jacques' premonition, though mistaken in its interpretation, would seem to show a particularly close psychic bond with his daughter. He is believed to have died shortly after Joan—it was said, of great sorrow upon learning of her martyrdom.

Isabelle d'Arc was also known as Isabelle Romée, which was a title given to those who had made a pilgrimage to Rome, but it is unlikely that Isabelle had ever made the journey, and she may have only inherited the title from an earlier family member.

Isabelle lived until 1458, her later years being spent in Orléans on a pension granted to her by the city, in gratitude for Joan's actions in raising the siege. In 1455, when approaching the age of 70, and in failing health, she had to appear in Paris at the cathedral of Notre Dame, with sons Pierre and Jean, as petitioner to the papal authority for Joan's rehabilitation in the eyes of Church and state.

The testimony of many of the surviving villagers of Domremy for the Rehabilitation proceedings, which were held in the tiny village church dedicated to St Remy, has given us a very detailed picture of Joan's childhood. Some of her godfathers and godmothers, of which there were several in those days before parish registers and other records were kept, testified to the worthiness of her parents who, as good Catholics, had taught Joan the basic tenets of the Church.

A local priest, Henri Arnoul, testified to Joan's devout nature, and said that she used to confess 'gladly and often', and 'when she was at church, she would be bowed before the Cross with her hands clasped and sometimes with her eyes raised and her face turned to the Crucifix and the Blessed Virgin'.

Perrin Drappier, who was the churchwarden of Domremy, testified that 'Joan the Maid was a chaste, simple and modest girl, who went to church often and confessed often; and when I forgot to ring the bells for Compline, Joan used to scold me, and she even promised to give me a present of some little cakes if I would be punctual in future.'

Joan's childhood friends also gave testimony of their memories of her. Colin, a farmer, remembered that she went gladly to church, and on Saturday afternoons would go with her sister and other women of the village to the hermitage of Our Lady of Bermont, carrying candles. He spoke of her religious devotions and said that she was so pious that he and some other village lads used to tease her about it.

Simonin Musnier, another farmer, who was brought up in the house next door to Joan, also spoke of her deeply religious nature. He said she tended the sick villagers and gave alms to the poor, and 'when I was ill as a child, Joan came to comfort me'.

Joan's dearest friend was Hauviette, who testified to Joan's 'good, sweet and simple nature', and said that Joan often blushed when people spoke to her about her devotion to her religious duties. She said she was frequently in the d'Arc household and remembered Joan's diligence to the household chores and of seeing her watching her father's flocks in the fields.

As in all typical village communities, the Domremy children had their simple leisure pursuits. Situated near the village was a large and ancient beech, whose branches reached almost to the ground. Called the Ladies' Tree, because the local ladies of the manor sometimes walked there, it was also known as the Fairies' Tree, and was believed by some to be the dwelling place of nature spirits. Close by was a spring, the Fontaine aux Rains, which was said to have healing powers, where the children would gather on Laetare Sunday, or Fountains Sunday, to make garlands of flowers and hang them from the branches of the tree; they would sing and dance around it, and afterwards eat their bread and drink from the spring.

Another, more serious activity took place when, together with her sister and their friends, Joan would walk the two miles or so to the chapel of Notre Dame de Bermont, situated deep in the wooded hills above Domremy's neighbouring village, Greux. Here they would light their candles and make little offerings of flowers to the statue of the Virgin, and quench their thirst at the ancient well of St Thiébault. Joan often went alone to the chapel, her devotion to which caused another of her friends, Mengette, also to tell her that she was being too pious.

Joan's exceptional piety was, therefore, well known to the villagers, but what remained hidden from everyone was the cause of that piety—for Joan possessed a great secret, the knowledge of which she would keep hidden for over four years, until, upon a mighty spiritual command, she would finally reveal it to the world.

★ ★ ★

Although in a relatively isolated position, Domremy was on a main trade route and there were many travellers passing through the village who brought news of events in the rest of France and report on the ongoing conflict between the two royal houses and the war with England. Events far away did, to some extent, influence life in Joan's village, and she stated at her trial that fights would even break out between the children of Domremy and those of its neighbour, Maxey, as Domremy considered itself supporters of the Dauphin and the Armagnac party, whereas Maxey supported the opposing faction, the Burgundian, which had sided with the English.

Joan's life followed its familiar course in Domremy until the year 1424, when an event occurred, which, because of its almost unbelievable nature, has so intrigued and mystified human minds down the ages—the first appearance to Joan of the great spiritual Being known to the western world as the Archangel Michael. At her trial she was repeatedly questioned about this event, which she described to her judges in these beautifully simple and moving words:

> When I was in my thirteenth year, I had a voice from God to help me govern my conduct. And the first time I was very much afraid. And came this voice about the hour of noon, in the summertime, in my father's garden ... I heard the voice on the right-hand side, towards the church; and rarely do I hear it without a brightness ... It is usually a great light ... The voice was sent to me by God and after I had thrice heard the voice, I knew that it was the voice of an angel ...

But she did, initially, doubt the nature of the voice:

> The first time I was only a child and was afraid, but afterwards St Michael taught me and showed me and proved to me that I must believe firmly that it was him. I knew who he was by his speech and by the language of the angels.

Questioned as to how she knew they were angels, she replied:

> I believed it quite quickly and I had the will to believe it. When St Michael came to me, he told me that St Catherine and St Margaret would come to me and that I should act by their advice, because they were ordered to lead me in what I had to do, and that I should believe in what they would say to me, as it was by Our Lord's command... And I should conduct myself well, and go habitually to church. And later the voice told me of the great pity that was in the realm of France and that I, Joan, should come into France... twice and thrice a week that I must go away and I would not bear to stay where I was... I should raise the siege laid to the city of Orléans and have the Dauphin crowned in the cathedral at Reims, and drive the English out of France.

Regarding Joan's 'Voices', as she collectively called her Heavenly Counsel, one of the closest of her entourage, her squire, Jean d'Aulon, who was with her throughout her mission, testified that Joan had told him:

> ... her Heavenly Counsel were three, of whom she said one always remained with her, another went away but came often to see her, and the third was he with whom the two others always consulted.

The two saints, Catherine and Margaret, were believed to be the Christian heroines of Alexandria and Antioch, who had defied the authorities of their times and suffered martyrdom as a result. A comparison has been drawn between Catherine's brilliant refutation of the pagan sages and Joan's similar experiences with her judges. Both saints were known to fifteenth-century Catholicism as patrons and protectors of young women, although little is actually known of their lives so long ago, which have become interwoven with legends of other early Christian martyrs.

Of the two saints, Margaret is mentioned less frequently by Joan. Catherine appears to have been the one who was always with her—certainly during all the most important events of her mission. In the later periods of Joan's waning fortunes and during her imprisonment, she said both saints were constantly with her.

Whatever the true identities of the saints, it is interesting to note that we have here an example of earlier members of humanity working from the spiritual worlds into human life. In this connection, Joan also spoke of her knowledge that two former Kings of France, Charlemagne and Louis IX—St Louis—were involved in the events then taking place on earth at the time; with these two great figures of earlier European history, we may picture members of the supersensible School of Michael involved in the destiny of France.

At her trial, Joan was questioned endlessly for a description of the two saints, but she said that, although she always saw them 'in the same form', she knew nothing of their apparel. When asked what part of them she saw, she answered, 'the face, and their heads are richly crowned'. She recognized them by their voices and said they spoke most excellently and beautifully, and she knew one from the other by the greeting each gave her. When questioned for more details she often avoided answering, and it is apparent that when she did answer, she did so unwillingly and then only under the greatest pressure.

Joan was also cross-examined in order to obtain a description of Michael but, even when exhausted by ill-treatment and illness during the months of her trial and subjected to the cleverest cross-questioning by her inquisitors, she was evasive and, in fact, very often scathing of their attempts to extract information about him.

She did speak of the radiance that preceded the voice of Michael and of the exaltation she felt as her consciousness became irradiated by his presence, but, she said, 'I am not going to tell you everything, but I do say to you that it is a beautiful voice, righteous and worthy—otherwise I am not bound to answer you, for I have not permission.' She said she saw Michael and his angels 'with my bodily eyes, as well as I am seeing you', but when asked as to his form, she said that he appeared 'in the form of a *prud'homme*'—an honourable and upright man. Later she was asked if he appeared to her naked—a common trick by the Inquisition to see if it could be proven that it was an appearance by the Devil—but she said, 'Do you think Our Lord has not the wherewithal to clothe him?' As the records state, 'as to his dress and the rest she would say nothing more'.

Joan often spoke to those around her of the hosts of angelic beings who accompanied Michael, and of their appearance and assistance during various battles, when she would indicate their presence to those who could not see them. As a number of witnesses testified, however, most people readily believed her, because of the great upliftment they experienced when she spoke, and the inspiration which radiated from her. Some did experience their presence; as she said, 'The King and some of his Council at Chinon saw and heard them, and knew their nature.'

★ ★ ★

It is important to note that Joan was not an ecstatic—all her spiritual experiences took place in full waking consciousness; even solitude was not necessary, although she preferred to be at a distance from people. Even so, in the din and chaos of the battlefield she frequently received her heavenly guidance to enable her to act in a crucial situation.

This is what Rudolf Steiner says about the nature of her clairvoyance and her spiritual experiences:

> ...following on what mankind has developed in the Intellectual Soul age, what has been developed and elaborated through our ego, what we are in a position to take in from the impressions of the outer world by dint of our own activity, must be carried upwards and interwoven into what is still to come in later times, Manas, or Spirit-Self. This, however, will not be until the sixth epoch which gives promise that mankind will then be in a position to bear upwards into higher regions of existence what has been unfolded through the outer impressions received by the ego through the senses. In this fifth culture-epoch we are in a position only to set about giving a certain stamp to everything we acquire from outer impressions and from working on them—a certain stamp which will imbue everything with an impetus in the upward direction. In this respect we are in truth living in a period of transition.
>
> When the man of our times enters into relation with spiritual Powers, he can carry upwards what he experiences in the physical world through the work of his ego and the impressions it receives; he can give it all an upward orientation. Hence in personalities such as the Maid of Orléans, the revelations, the manifestations of those spiritual Powers who desire to speak to her, take place, to be sure, in the sphere to which she reaches, but something spreads itself in front

of these revelations, without actually detracting from their reality but giving them a particular form—the form arising from what the ego experiences here in the physical world. In other words: the Maid of Orléans had revelations, but she could not behold them with the direct vision of the people of ancient times; the mental pictures she had known in the physical world—pictures of the Virgin Mary, of the Archangel Michael, arising from her Christian conceptions—interposed themselves between her own egohood and the objective spiritual Powers.

There we have an example of how in spiritual matters we must distinguish between the objectivity of a revelation and the objectivity of a content of consciousness. The Maid of Orléans saw the Virgin Mary and the Archangel Michael in the form of a certain picture. We must not conceive these pictures to be the spiritual reality itself; nor must we ascribe direct objectivity to the form they take. Revelations from the spiritual world did indeed come to the Maid of Orléans, revelations which in the sixth culture-epoch—and not until then—man will be able to see in the form in which they should be seen in the post-Atlantean epoch. But although the Maid of Orléans did not see this true form, it did come down towards her. She brought the religious conceptions of her day to meet these revelations, clothed them as it were in this imagery; her world of mental images was evoked by the spiritual Power. The revelation is therefore to be regarded as objective. Even if in our time someone can show that subjective elements make their way into a revelation from the spiritual world, even if we cannot regard the actual picture which the person in question forms for himself as objective, even if it is only a veil—we must not for that reason assert that the objective revelations themselves are veils. They are objective; but their content is conjured forth from the soul. We must distinguish between the objectivity of that content and the objectivity of the facts which come from the spiritual world.

The Maid of Orléans is therefore a personality already working entirely in the spirit of our own epoch, when everything that we can produce on the foundation of our outer impressions must be directed upward to the spiritual.

* * *

From 1424 until the early part of 1428, we know from Joan's testimony that she was receiving guidance and instruction from her Heavenly Counsel, and that this was her probationary period, relating to her conduct and behaviour:

> From that first time when Michael came to me, I vowed my virginity to God, for as long as it should please Him. From the time that I knew I was to go into France, I gave myself as little as possible to games and play.

In the middle of 1428 a number of events took place, the significance of which showed an urgent need for the start of Joan's mission. Anglo-Burgundian forces were threatening to besiege the city of Orléans, while at the same time the loyal outpost of Vaucouleurs was also threatened with attack. The surrounding area was subjected to frequent raids and Domremy suffered a fierce assault when much of the village was burned down, rendering it uninhabitable. The entire population fled to the safety of Neufchâteau, where Joan and her family lodged at an inn in the town that was run by a woman known as La Rousse on account of her red hair. Joan helped her with the routine daily tasks, but during her trial accusations were made that the inn was a place of ill-repute and the judges tried to twist the evidence in an attempt to show that Joan had led an immoral life while living there.

It was during the stay at Neufchâteau that Joan had to travel to Toul, some 20 miles away, to appear before the ecclesiastical court to answer a suit for breach of promise, from which she was entirely exonerated. It would appear that her parents, sensing that their daughter was not following the familiar path to courtship and marriage of the other village girls of her age, had promised her in marriage to a young man in the vicinity. At her trial Joan was most emphatic that the betrothal had been made without her consent.

Eventually, when the danger to Domremy had passed, the villagers were able to return, and the threat of siege to Vaucouleurs was lifted when an armistice was agreed.

Although Joan had kept the secret of her inner life hidden up to this time, as the start of her mission drew near she hinted about it to a young friend in the village, Michel Lebuin. He must have been greatly mystified at the time, but would later testify: 'Joan told me herself, on the eve of St John the Baptist, that there lived a maid between Coussey and Vaucouleurs who would have the King of France anointed within a year.'

On 12 October the siege of Orléans began, when a strong army headed by John, Earl of Salisbury, attacked the outer fortifications of the city.

Joan's Heavenly Counsel now became more and more insistent that she should begin her mission. Her instructions were to go to Robert de Baudricourt, Captain of the garrison at Vaucouleurs, and convince him that he must send her to the Dauphin, who at that time was residing in the château of Chinon in the lower part of the Loire, some 300 miles away.

But how was this seemingly impossible task to be achieved? How could a young girl, who had never ventured further than the familiar surroundings of her village, attempt such a journey, as she was now instructed to do? At first Joan resisted the urgings of her Voice: 'I answered it that I was a poor girl who knew not how to ride nor lead in war.'

Finally, the continued insistence of her Voice convinced Joan that she must leave Domremy, and she eventually found the means whereby she was able to undertake the first stage of her mission.

Joan's excuse for leaving home came in the form of her cousin Jeanne, the wife of Durand Laxart, a farm labourer, living in the village of Burey-le-Petit, some three miles from Vaucouleurs. Jeanne was expecting a baby at the beginning of 1429, and Joan seized the opportunity presented by the confinement by offering to stay in their home and help with the housework. Her offer was accepted and Laxart went to Domremy to take Joan back with him.

As Laxart was 15 years older than Joan, she always called him 'uncle', and they seem to have had a close relationship. Even so, this simple man must have been astounded when Joan told him the real reason behind her visit. In his testimony for the Rehabilitation proceedings he stated that Joan had told him that she had to go into France and have the Dauphin crowned, and she quoted to him an old prophecy which had long been current in the region: 'Has it not been said that France will be ruined by a woman and afterwards be restored by a virgin?' Laxart must have been utterly taken aback by Joan's statement, but her inspiring manner and the passion with which she always spoke—so often to be noted by those who were associated with her throughout her mission—apparently convinced him that he should take her to Vaucouleurs to deliver her message to Robert de Baudricourt. Although he may still have felt a certain amount of trepidation at the thought of the impending meeting with such an important man, the pair nevertheless set off on their short journey on or about 6 January 1429.

Asked at her trial if it was not a great shock to her parents when they learned of her departure, Joan replied:

> My Voices did not oblige me to hold this secret and would have been satisfied that I tell them, had it not been for the pain it would have caused them. In all other things I did obey my father and my mother, save in this leaving them, but afterwards I wrote to them and they gave me their forgiveness. But since God commanded it, it had to be ... had I had a hundred fathers and a hundred mothers and had I been a king's daughter, I should have departed.

2 Vaucouleurs

Upon their arrival in Vaucouleurs, Laxart arranged for Joan to lodge in the house of a couple with whom he was friendly, the wheelwright Henri Le Royer and his wife Catherine. During the weeks Joan stayed in their home Catherine became very fond of her and would testify at the Rehabilitation proceedings to her 'simplicity, her gentleness and her respectful conduct'. Of Joan's impatience to begin her mission, Catherine said, 'Joan ardently desired this, and the time lagged for her as for a woman great with child.'

Joan was eventually granted an audience with Robert de Baudricourt and, together with Laxart, she eagerly set off, following the steep hill from the town which led to the Captain's headquarters in the château-fortress, for her first meeting with him. When she entered the great hall, Joan lost no time in delivering the message from her Heavenly Counsel, addressing de Baudricourt in her usual forthright manner: 'I am come in the name of my Lord to ask that you send me to the Dauphin, for I must tell him to be patient and not make war with his enemies, as the Lord will send him aid before mid-Lent.'

De Baudricourt, obviously greatly astonished at Joan's bold statement, asked her, 'And who is your Lord?' At Joan's reply, 'My Lord is the King of Heaven,' he must have thought that this young peasant girl, standing before him in her red dress, was quite mad, and he dismissed her, ordering Laxart to give her a 'sound cuffing' and take her back to her father's house.

Following de Baudricourt's curt dismissal, there was nothing more to be done for the time being, and a disappointed and very frustrated Joan returned with Laxart to his house at Burey-le-Petit for a short time.

While Joan was away, news of her abortive meeting with de Baudricourt had begun to circulate, and there was growing interest and speculation about her among the townspeople of Vaucouleurs. After the meeting, an angry Joan had spoken passionately to Catherine Le Royer about the urgency of her mission, and repeated to her hostess the prophecy she had given to Laxart. In her testimony

Catherine stated: 'When Joan saw that Robert would not escort her, she said—I heard her say it—that she must go to the place where the Dauphin was: "Have you not heard the prophecy that France was to be ruined by a woman and restored by a virgin from the marches of Lorraine?" Having heard that, I was flabbergasted.' Although Catherine would have been familiar with this well-known prophecy, the fervour of Joan's words brought the sudden realization that Joan was actually declaring herself to be the virgin of the prophecy. (When Joan's fame began to spread, the prophecy became widely known in the rest of France, and it was generally believed that the infamous Isabeau de Bavière was the woman who had fulfilled the first half of the prophecy.)

In the medieval world prophecies abounded, and many had found their way into popular folklore. One that was widespread in France was the prophecy of the visionary Marie d'Avignon, which she made to the Dauphin's father, Charles VI, many years before Joan appeared. Marie had experienced many visions concerning the sufferings of France, in particular, the one in which she had been shown many suits of armour. Afraid that she had to wear the armour and fight, she was told that it was not meant for her, but for a maid who would come afterwards and who would deliver the kingdom of France.

Another famous prophecy was that attributed to Merlin, which spoke of 'a marvellous Maid, who will come from the *Nemus Canutum*, the Ancient or Oak Wood, for the healing of nations'. The prophecy became associated with Joan and recognized as the Bois Chenu, the ancient oak wood covering the hill above Domremy.

Joan returned to Vaucouleurs to find herself the object of intense interest, and now met the two men who were to be her first champions and faithful companions on the journey to the Dauphin at Chinon. Jean de Nouillempont, known as Jean de Metz, and Bertrand de Poulengy were squires in the service of de Baudricourt at the garrison in the town.

The 57-year-old de Metz, gave his lengthy testimony to the Rehabilitation proceedings about this first meeting with Joan:

When Joan the Maid came to Vaucouleurs I saw her in a red dress, poor and worn.

Then, somewhat condescendingly, but kindly, he asked her:

> *Ma mie*, what are you doing here? Is it not fated that the King shall be driven from his kingdom, and that we shall all turn English? And the Maid answered me: 'I am come here to this royal town to speak to Robert de Baudricourt, to ask him to escort me, or have me escorted, to the King, but he pays no attention to me nor to my words. But all the same, before mid-Lent, I must be with the King, even if I have to wear my feet to the knees. For there is no one on earth, be he king, or duke ... or anyone else, who can recover the kingdom for France and he will have no help except through me, although I would rather stay with my poor mother and spin, for this is not my station. But I must go and I must do it, for my Lord wishes me to perform this deed.' And when I asked her who her Lord was, she said that he was God.

De Metz was immediately won over by Joan's impassioned words:

> And then I, Jean, who testify to this had great confidence in the Maid and I was fired by her sayings with love for her, divine as I believe, and I promised the Maid, putting my hands in hers as a gesture of fealty that, God helping, I would lead her to the Dauphin. And I asked her when she wanted to go, and she answered, 'Rather today than tomorrow, and rather tomorrow than later.'

The 63-year-old de Poulengy, who testified similarly, appears to have known the d'Arc family, and he added that he 'was often in their house'.

Joan made another visit to de Baudricourt, again without success, but the Captain must have begun to have some doubts, as he sent a letter to the Dauphin requesting his opinion as to whether Joan should be sent to him or not.

Joan was now becoming ever more frustrated at the delay in starting her mission, and she decided to take matters into her own hands. This was a surprising decision because, as she stated at her trial: 'Robert twice refused and repulsed me, and the third time he received me and gave me men. The Voice had told me that this would so happen.' As she usually obeyed her Heavenly Counsel without question, it can only have been her intense frustration that made her act against their advice.

Again, the dependable Laxart was asked to help. At Joan's urging, he and a friend, Jacques Alain, purchased a horse for her. After Joan had exchanged her red peasant's dress for a suit of her uncle's clothes, the three set off from Vaucouleurs one afternoon in late January. As they rode on, and with night approaching, Joan decided to stop at Saint-Nicolas-de-Septfonds, a famous place of pilgrimage, where there was a chapel in the forest and where she could offer a prayer for the success of her journey. It was while praying before the oak-carved figure of Christ that she realized the futility of departing on her mission without the help which her Voices had promised her, and she decided she must return to Vaucouleurs.

Upon returning to the town, Joan received a message from Duke Charles of Lorraine, requesting her to visit him, under the promise of a safe conduct, at his residence in Nancy, a distance of about 50 miles, a journey on which she was accompanied by de Metz. The Duke was very old and suffering from an incurable disease, but having heard of this amazing young Maid, perhaps thought that she might be able to cure him. When he questioned Joan about this, she told him quite frankly that she did not know if he would recover his health, but she advised him to give up his mistress, Alison Dumay (with whom he had had five bastards), and be reconciled with his long-suffering wife, Marguerite of Bavaria! She also asked him for men-at-arms to accompany her to Chinon, promising in return to pray for his health to be restored. The soldiers were not forthcoming, but the Duke appears not to have been offended by Joan's bold approach, as he gave her a black horse, and four gold francs for the expenses of her journey.

In early February Joan was back in Vaucouleurs, and at her third meeting with de Baudricourt she was to give him some amazing news: 'In God's name, you delay too long in sending me, for this very day the noble Dauphin has suffered great loss near Orléans, and will suffer yet more if you do not send me speedily to him.'

She was referring to what became known as the Battle of the Herrings, which took place on 12 February at Rouvray. Jean Dunois, the Bastard of Orléans, had attempted to stop a convoy of provisions—mainly salt-fish for Lent—from reaching the English besiegers but was defeated in a counter-attack by Sir John Fastolf's army. This was the last attempt to raise the siege before Joan's arrival.

Joan's awareness of this event, on the day it was taking place hundreds of miles away, is one example of the many psychic gifts she possessed. There are many instances of her clairvoyant and clairaudient powers, and she had the ability to foresee and prophesy significant future events, both in the immediate and in the distant future. In the heat of the battle of Jargeau, she saved the life of the Duke of Alençon, by warning him to move from the exact spot where a little while later another man was killed by enemy artillery. At her trial she prophesied the fall of Paris to the French in 1436, and (by a year) the French triumph at the battle of Formigny in 1450, which resulted in the recovery of Normandy, leading to the revival of French fortunes and the decline of English domination in France. She predicted the two occasions when she would be wounded in battle: at the siege of Orléans and before the walls of Paris. In the early stages of her mission she told the lethargic Dauphin and others to 'use me well, for I shall last but a year'.

★ ★ ★

Rudolf Steiner has compared Joan's prophetic powers with those of the sibyls of the ancient world. The sibyllism that existed in a rightful manner until into the third epoch as a lawful means of spiritual inspiration, working in and through the astral body, gradually became more chaotic in its nature. Sibyllism then declined in order that the philosophy of the Greek age could arise. Later, the sibylline forces in men's souls were transformed by Christ by the Mystery of Golgotha. Rudolf Steiner describes Joan as an example of a sibyl transformed by the Christ Impulse, and he calls her 'the Christ-filled sibyl'.

★ ★ ★

Joan's revelation does not appear to have convinced de Baudricourt, but at this point the royal messenger, Colet de Vienne, arrived from Chinon, bringing the Dauphin's response to de Baudricourt's request. The answer was that provided the Captain was satisfied as to Joan's character, and that she was no sorceress, inspired by evil forces, he could send her at once to Chinon.

De Baudricourt made one last attempt to satisfy himself as to Joan's credibility and, as Catherine Le Royer testified, he arrived at her house accompanied by the parish priest, Jean Fournier, insisting that Joan be exorcised. In her reply to the words of the exorcism, 'If thou art an evil thing, depart far from me; if thou art holy, draw near,' Joan, on her knees, protested: 'This is not fair of you; you know there is no evil in me, since you heard me in confession.'

With de Baudricourt now as convinced as he would ever be, he took the decision to have Joan escorted to Chinon without further delay. It is recorded that the people of Vaucouleurs presented Joan with 'a black doublet attached to black hose by 20 points (laces), a dark grey cloak, a black cap with chaperon (hood), and leather boots with spurs'. She was also presented with a dagger. Catherine Le Royer cut Joan's hair *à l'ecuelle*, that is, short above the ears, in the style of the soldiers of the day. De Baudricourt provided her with a horse and a sword. De Metz and de Poulengy were to bear the expenses of the journey.

One evening in February (the exact date is disputed by various Johannic scholars), as dusk fell in the courtyard of the château, the townspeople of Vaucouleurs gathered to witness Joan's departure. After de Baudricourt had taken an oath from de Metz and de Poulengy that they would guard her well on the journey and deliver her safely to the Dauphin, the two men, with their servants, were joined by Richard the Archer and Colet de Vienne, who had in his keeping the letters of introduction from de Baudricourt. They all mounted their horses, and de Baudricourt spoke his famous words of farewell—the tone of which appeared to indicate a lingering scepticism in his mind, about the wisdom of sending this bold young girl with her fantastic claims to no less a personage than his liege lord, the Dauphin: '*Va, Va, et advienne que pourra!*'—'Go, Go, and come what may!'

As the party rode out of the château, through the Porte de France, Joan turned to the crowd gathered in the courtyard, and said: 'I fear not, for my Lord will clear the way for me to the Dauphin, for this was I born...'

At the start of their eleven-day journey, the party spent their first night in Saint-Urbain, where Joan was accommodated in the guest house of the great abbey. Travelling most of the way through Anglo-Burgundian held territory, they rode mainly at night, sleeping in woods by day. On the long journey through hostile territory they were in constant danger of ambush or attack, either from the enemy or from marauding bands of robbers who roamed the countryside.

On the way, de Metz and de Poulengy often questioned Joan about her mission and in their testimony said they were greatly inspired when she spoke about her Voices. De Poulengy said that, in spite of the many alarms on the road, Joan always reassured them that they would reach their goal safely. He said 'she was always such a virtuous girl that she seemed like a saint'. De Metz testified: 'Both Bertrand and I slept each night with her. The Maid slept beside us without taking off her doublet and hose and, as for me, I was in such awe of her that I would not have dared go near her; and I tell you on my oath that I never had any desire or carnal feelings for her.'

Joan often expressed her wish to hear Mass, but it was not possible because of the ever-present danger on the way. When they eventually reached Auxerre, although it was Burgundian in sympathy, it was felt that it was sufficiently safe to stop briefly in the Benedictine monastery outside the town where, much to her great joy, Joan was finally able to hear the longed-for Mass.

Nearing the end of their journey, the party reached the village of Sainte-Catherine-de-Fierbois, where a chapel in the woods contained a shrine dedicated to Joan's special saint.

After spending the night in the sanctuary, Joan prayed next morning in the chapel and heard three Masses. Before leaving, she sent a messenger ahead to Chinon to announce her impending arrival, and the party set off on the final stage of their journey. Following the right bank of the Vienne, they came in sight of the imposing château, magnificently poised on top of the clifflike hill above the town, arriving about noon. De Metz summed up their journey: 'And thus we took her to the King, to the place of Chinon.'

3   Chinon

Joan arrived in Chinon, either on Wednesday, 23 February or Sunday, 6 March (authorities differ as to the dates), and was lodged for two days with a 'worthy widow' in a house situated on the Carrefour du Grand-Carroi, at the foot of the steep hill leading to the château.

On the second day, 'at a high hour' (around eight o'clock in the evening), Joan and her escort rode up the hill for her long-awaited meeting with the Dauphin. As she was about to pass over the drawbridge there was a disturbance, when one of the guards shouted, 'Is that the Maid? *Jarnidieu*! (I deny God!), if I had her for a night, I would not return her in that condition!' Hearing these words, Joan replied, 'Ha! *en nom Dieu*, you deny Him and you so near your death!' The reported outcome was that, within the hour, the man fell into the moat and was drowned.

When Joan entered the château, she was conducted by Charles de Bourbon, Count of Clermont, to the Great Hall where some three hundred members of the Dauphin's court were assembled. Upon entering the crowded chamber, she was met by the blazing light of torches, and she would describe the effect this spectacle had upon her to the judges at her trial: 'There were more than three hundred knights and more that 50 torches, as well as the spiritual light...' It seems unlikely that such a great number of knights were present at a court so impoverished as that of the Dauphin, but there were certainly many of his high-ranking officers there, including his Chamberlain, Georges de la Trémoille, Regnault de Chartres, the Archbishop of Reims and Raoul de Gaucourt, the Governor of Orléans, who had come to Chinon to give the Dauphin the latest news about the siege.

The meeting of Joan with the Dauphin has been told in a number of ways, that he hid among his courtiers or placed another on his throne, but it would seem that when Joan entered the hall he was not in a prominent position. He may have wished to get a glimpse of this strange young girl before she saw him and, forewarned, to test her to see if she could really recognize him. As Joan would later testify, 'I knew him among the others by the counsel of my Voices which revealed him to me.' She went straight to him and, kneeling before him, said, '*Gentil Dauphin, j'ai nom Jehanne la Pucelle*, and the King of Heaven commands that through me you be anointed and crowned in the city of Reims as a lieutenant of the King of Heaven, who is King of France.' She then told him that she was sent to raise the siege of Orléans and, further, that she would give him a 'sign' which would prove to him that her mission was of divine origin.

Intrigued but not entirely convinced by Joan's declaration, the Dauphin left the noise and clamour of the hall and withdrew with Joan to the privacy of his chapel. When they emerged some time later it was noted by those present that the Dauphin's demeanour was considerably changed, one witness stating that he appeared 'radiant'; Charles afterwards said that Joan had told him of 'things so secret that no mortal but himself could possibly have known, except by divine revelation'.

What actually took place between Joan and the Dauphin at their secluded meeting, and by what means she was able to convince him that he was the true heir to the throne of France, has consistently intrigued all Johannic students, who have studied this episode closely, and there has been much speculation about the nature of this 'sign' which Joan gave to the Dauphin. Most writers on the subject have concluded that it relates to an unspoken prayer, made by the Dauphin in the solitude of his chapel, before Joan's arrival in Chinon. Because Joan repeated his prayer to him, it has been generally agreed that this apparent miracle was the 'sign' by which he came to believe in her and in the divine origin of her mission.

Another attempt to solve the mystery of the 'sign' has its origin in a session of the Trial of Condemnation, when on 13 March 1431 Joan was subjected to a lengthy interrogation by the judges about the sign she had given to the Dauphin—an episode which has become known as 'the allegory of the crown', and a subject of much debate by biographers. Although she was at first reluctant to answer, Joan eventually replied that the sign was an angel who had presented the Dauphin with a crown, thereby assuring him of his right to the throne of France.

The judges continued to press Joan about the nature of the sign, and writers who have investigated this episode are generally in agreement that she tried to evade further cross-examination by taking refuge in a fantastic allegory about the angel and the crown, which she then confused with the Dauphin's crowning at Reims. In this attempt to interpret the 'allegory', the assumption has been made that Joan was simply elaborating her own role, and that she herself was the 'angel' who had presented the Dauphin with his crown—which, of course, she had.

Although some writers on the subject are convinced that this is the explanation of the allegory of the crown, others have expressed dissatisfaction with both attempts to interpret the 'sign', and have also admitted that it may never be possible to fathom its true nature.

However, the present writer believes that the true meaning of the 'sign' can be found in the trial session of 13 March, and that previous attempts to decipher the mystery by intellectual conjecture alone have, by their very nature, resulted only in a superficial interpretation of the 'sign'. As Rudolf Steiner pointed out, people write biographies today without any idea that Spiritual Powers are at work in human destiny, and the same may be said of attempts at interpretation without this vital recognition. This is why there has been failure to recognize that Joan's testimony reveals the deeply esoteric nature of the events which took place at her meeting with the Dauphin. Therefore, the solution to the mystery of the 'sign' can only be found by recognizing the significance of spiritual intervention and guidance in crucial events of human history and development. (For a detailed account and explanation of the 'sign', see Chapter 12.)

The day after Joan's audience with the Dauphin, she met a man who was to become a devoted friend and staunch ally, whom she would always refer to as her *beau duc*. Jean, Duke of Alençon, a prince of the blood royal and cousin of the Dauphin, was away on a hunting expedition when he heard of Joan's arrival at Chinon. Upon being informed of the purpose of her visit, he immediately returned and was introduced to Joan who, upon learning who he was, declared, 'You are very welcome; the more the royal blood of France is gathered together, the better it will be.' In his testimony for the Rehabilitation proceedings, he stated that he was impressed to see Joan on horseback one evening at Chinon, tilting with a lance, and with such ease that he was amazed at her proficiency, and made her a present of a horse. He later took her to visit his home at Saint-Florent-lès-Saumur, where his wife expressed her fears for his safety—he had only recently returned from five years' imprisonment in England, having been captured at the battle of Verneuil in 1424, and had paid a heavy ransom for his release—but Joan assured her that she need have no fear, as she would return him safely to her when their forthcoming battles were over.

Despite the Dauphin's initial belief in Joan and the euphoria he had experienced at their extraordinary meeting, some doubts appear to have crossed his mind about her credibility. As was usually the case, his weak and indecisive nature was influenced by doubts expressed by his dominating counsellors. They asked: was she really a virgin sent by God? Or was she a sorceress?—such women were believed to have intercourse with the Devil, and if this were the case, she could not be 'the Maid', as she claimed.

While these deliberations were taking place, Joan was lodged in the Tour de Coudray, a part of the château with its own history, as it was here, in 1308, that some of the Knights Templar had been imprisoned after their denunciation by King Philip the Fair on charges of heresy. Joan was given members of the household to serve her needs, and assigned a page, Louis de Coutes, a boy of about 14, who had been learning the profession of arms in the service of Raoul de Gaucourt. Louis lived in the tower by day, and in his testimony recalled his youthful curiosity about Joan: 'I often saw Joan on her knees praying, but I was never able to hear what she said, although she sometimes wept. At night she had women with her, and during her stay in the tower, many persons of high rank visited her, but I did not know what they said, as I always ran off when I saw them coming.' Louis would remain in Joan's service up to the time of the assault on Paris.

The Dauphin's advisers eventually reached the decision that Joan should be taken to Poitiers, to be examined by the learned doctors of the re-formed University of Paris, who were loyal to the Dauphin's cause and had been obliged to leave Paris and take refuge in Poitiers following the English occupation of the city. When Joan was informed of the reason for the visit, she said, '*En nom Dieu*, I shall have much difficulty there, but my Counsel will help me—let us go!' As her tone implies, she was impatient as always throughout her mission, to proceed to the next stage without delay. The Dauphin and his retinue accompanied Joan to Poitiers, where she was lodged in the house of Master Jean Rabateau, the Dauphin's privy councillor, who had been Advocate-General of the Parliament of Paris before the enforced withdrawal from the city.

Joan was subjected to lengthy questioning in a number of sessions during the three weeks she was in Poitiers, by theologians of the University and by other experts in canon and civil law. The President of the examining commission was the Archbishop of Reims, Regnault de Chartres—later to become Joan's bitter enemy, when events turned against her.

During one particularly notable session, Joan was questioned for two hours about her Voices, her departure for Vaucouleurs and her visit to the Dauphin at Chinon. Present on this occasion was Brother Seguin de Seguin, a member of the Order of Preaching Friars and professor of theology, who survived into old age to give his lengthy testimony 27 years later for the Rehabilitation proceedings. He testified about another member of his Order, Guillaume Aimeri, who had asked Joan if, as her Voices had told her, God wished to deliver the people of France from their enemies, why should it be necessary to fight, to which Joan replied, 'In God's name, the soldiers will fight, and God will give them the victory.'

Joan had become somewhat wearied by the long interrogation, and when Seguin began to question her again, she was impatient with him and quick to her defence. Seguin: 'I asked her in what language her Voices spoke, and she answered me, "A better one than yours!" Me, I spoke with a Limousin accent. And I asked her if she believed in God and she replied, "Yes, better than you." I then asked her how she could expect us to believe in her and advise the Dauphin to entrust her with soldiers, unless she could give us something more than her bare word on the matter, and she said, "I am not come to Poitiers to make signs, but lead me to Orléans and I will show you the sign I was sent to make!"'

Following this lively exchange Joan then repeated the reasons for her mission to the assembly. First, the siege of Orléans must be raised, after which the Dauphin would be crowned King at Reims; then Paris would be returned to the King, and Charles, Duke of Orléans, would return to France. (He had been captured at Agincourt in 1415 and remained a prisoner in England.) Seguin then testified: 'All this I have seen come to pass.'

The learned doctors were impressed by the way in which Joan gave her answers, replying with great conviction, and it was noted that she was moved to tears when describing how she had learned from her Voices 'that God had great pity on the realm of France'.

After enquiring further into Joan's life and her Christian beliefs, the theologians pronounced themselves satisfied with her and stated that, in their opinion, there was nothing to prevent the Dauphin from using her.

The documents of this enquiry, the so-called 'Book of Poitiers', have unfortunately never come to light. They may still lie in the archives of Poitiers, or elsewhere. There exists only a brief fragment, which states that the doctors had found 'no evil in her, but only goodness, humility, virginity, devoutness, honesty and simplicity'.

The atmosphere of this 'trial', though extremely searching and thorough, was conducted in a fair and open manner, and Joan had, in the main, always answered openly and freely. At the Trial of Condemnation, when she was subjected to harsh interrogation by her judges, she would often refer them back to her testimony at Poitiers, requests which were always denied, since they were bent on convicting her at all costs.

One further test remained. In order to confirm Joan's declaration of herself as 'Maid', it was necessary to discover if she was a virgin. For this purpose she was taken to Tours, to be examined by Yolande of Aragon, Queen of Sicily, and mother of the Dauphin's wife, Marie of Anjou. Yolande was a remarkable woman, and it is believed that she had earlier influenced the timid and vacillating Dauphin to take up the title 'King of France'. Politically active in the life of the court, she appears again in other important episodes during Charles VII's reign. Joan was duly examined by Yolande and two of the ladies of her household, who, 'having examined her in the secret parts of her body, found her to be a true and intact virgin'.

With all obstacles now removed, the way was clear for Joan's mission to begin, and she lost no time in setting about what she believed—perhaps somewhat naively—to be her first important task. Returning to Poitiers, she told Jean Erault, one of her examiners, 'I know not A from B, but if you have paper and ink, write what I shall tell you.' She then proceeded to dictate what must surely be the most impertinent letter ever to be addressed to a king—the first of three such letters she would send to the English.

Dated Tuesday of Holy Week, 22 March 1429, her lengthy admonition began: 'Jhesus Maria. King of England, and you, Duke of Bedford, who call yourself Regent of the Kingdom of France...,' and then addressing each of the English commanders by name, she demands they 'surrender to the Maid, who is sent here from God, the King of Heaven, the keys of all the good cities you have taken and violated in France. She is very ready to make peace, provided that you give up France and pay your accounts for having occupied her... Leave Orléans and return to your own country, for God's sake.' After continuing in a similar vein, the letter goes on: 'If you do not wish to believe this message from God through the Maid, then wherever we find you we will strike you and make such a *hahay* greater than any made in France for a thousand years.' The letter ends with Joan again requesting the Duke of Bedford to desist from further destruction, and even proposing that he and his army come to join hers in peace.

The reaction of the Duke of Bedford is not known, but this powerful man no doubt simply dismissed the haughty and imperious tone of Joan's letter as a huge bluff; he did not reply, and the siege of Orléans continued.

With the Dauphin's confidence in Joan now firmly established, he immediately began preparations for her to lead the army for the march on Orléans, and he instructed the Duke of Alençon to assemble a new army and make all the arrangements necessary for the raising of the siege. Meanwhile, after a brief return to Chinon, Joan was escorted to Tours where, as the record states, the Dauphin had arranged for 'a harness to be fitted for her body'—a suit of 'white' armour, so called because it was devoid of ornamentation. Payment for this was made 'To the Master Armourer, for a complete harness for the Maid, *100 livres tournois*'.

The next stage was to establish Joan's military household, in accordance with the high rank now bestowed upon her. First to be appointed was her squire, Jean d'Aulon, who would be constantly at her side throughout her mission, and was captured at Compiègne and imprisoned with her.

Her chaplain, Jean Pasquerel, an Augustinian friar, came to join her. For Joan he was the most important addition; he was to share in all the important moments of her life, always at her side to hear her confessions and minister to the army until the time of her capture. He had been on a pilgrimage to the shrine of Notre Dame du Puy at the time Joan left Vaucouleurs, and had met her mother there; it was she who had persuaded him to go in search of Joan and try to join her company. His lengthy testimony for the Rehabilitation is one of the finest and most detailed accounts.

Heralds and servants were assigned to Joan and, in addition to Louis de Coutes, another page, Raymond, who would be killed during the assault on Paris.

Joan's brothers Jean and Pierre also joined her at this point, as did the companions of her journey to Chinon, Jean de Metz and Bertrand de Poulengy.

A standard and pennon were made to Joan's instructions, the design of which she said had been imparted to her by her Heavenly Counsel, who had told her to have the King of Heaven painted upon it, and to 'bear it boldly'. She regarded the standard as the most important item of her military equipment. It was made for her by 'Hauves Poulnoir'— as he was known to the French—his actual name was Hamish Power, a Scotsman who lived in Tours. He was paid *25 livres tournois*, 'for painting and providing materials for a great standard and a small for the Maid'.

Descriptions of the standard differ, but it was made of either stiffened white silk or satin, with a gold silk fringe and a background sprinkled with gold fleurs-de-lis; it bore the inscription, *Jhesus Maria*, and the main design was a representation of Christ in Glory holding the world in his hand, and on each side an angel kneeling, one of whom presents a lily, which Christ is blessing. On the reverse was the figure of the Virgin Mary and a shield with the arms of France supported by two angels. (Although there has been much speculation as to Joan's status on the battlefield, in the fifteenth century the white standard was carried only by the commander of the army, the captains bearing their own insignia in a variety of colours.) The small standard referred to was actually a pennon, to be carried by a page, which depicted the Annunciation, with an angel presenting the Virgin Mary with a lily.

Before the attack on Orléans, when the army was assembled at Blois, Joan asked Jean Pasquerel to have a banner made, which depicted the crucified Christ with Mary and St John at the foot of the Cross. Of this banner, Pasquerel said, 'Twice a day Joan made me assemble all the priests to sing anthems and hymns to St Mary, and she exhorted all the soldiers to come to this gathering and make confession.' This banner was always carried by the priests at the head of the army.

Mention is also made in the records of a pennon which Joan is said to have adopted for her own private use; depicted on a blue background was a white dove, holding in its beak a scroll with the words *De par le Roy du Ciel*; beneath this was a device consisting of a crown upheld by a sword and flanked by two fleurs-de-lis. (This device appears to be the basic design for the coat-of-arms later given by Charles VII to Joan's family upon their ennoblement.)

All that now remained to complete Joan's military equipment was a sword and, much to the amazement of those around her, Joan declared that she knew of the very sword she must have; her Voices had told her to send to Sainte-Catherine-de-Fierbois—the place where she had rested on her journey to Chinon—where the sword would be found, buried somewhere near the altar of the church. An armourer from Tours was sent to Fierbois, bearing a letter requesting the clergy to search for the sword, which was eventually found, covered in rust, in an old reliquary behind the altar. When the sword was cleaned, it was found to be engraved with five crosses, which Joan had said would be the means of identifying it. (Despite speculation about the significance of this symbol, no satisfactory explanation has ever been given.)

A chapel had existed on the site at Fierbois since before the eighth century, and many votive offerings of arms and armour had been made there over the centuries by soldiers giving thanks after battle. Charles Martel, the earlier, great hero of France and grandfather of Charlemagne, was known to have left a sword there after his victory over the Saracens at Poitiers in 732. When news of the discovery of Joan's sword began to circulate, many believed that it was the actual sword left by Martel at the shrine.

The sword was presented to Joan by the clergy of Fierbois in a sheath of red velvet, and another, even more beautiful one in cloth of gold came from the city of Tours. When Joan was questioned on the matter at her trial, she said, 'I myself had another one made of right strong leather. I always wore that sword until the assault on Paris.' After the failed attempt against the city, Joan left the sword as a votive offering in the church of Saint-Denis. She also stated, when asked which she liked better, her standard or her sword, 'I bore the standard when we went against the enemy to avoid killing anyone. I have never killed anyone.' (The only time Joan is known to have drawn her sword was when she chased a camp-follower. Louis de Coutes witnessed the event: 'She did not strike the woman, but gently chastised her and told her to leave the camp; otherwise, she would do something to her that she would not like.')

With the addition of a small battleaxe, Joan was now fully equipped. She was presented with a handsome black charger, the first of three warhorses she is known to have possessed. At the triumphal entry into Orléans she rode a white charger, and when captured at Compiègne she was riding a dapple grey demi-courser.

As news about Joan began to spread, her appearance was described in a number of contemporary reports, from which we learn that she had dark hair, a 'low, sweet and compelling voice', and a bright red birthmark behind her right ear. Her squire, d'Aulon, whose duty was to dress her in her armour, said she was *'belle et bien formée'*—attractive and well-formed. Her height was about 5 ft 2 in. The details of her measurements are known from the extant fifteenth-century account books of the city of Orléans, from which her measurements were taken by Adrien Harmand, a French master tailor, who published them in an illustrated volume in 1929 that showed reconstructions of her armour and costumes, including that of the Orléans livery granted to her to wear at the coronation of Charles VII.

A detailed account of her bearing and mannerisms was given by Perceval de Boulainvilliers, Chamberlain of the French court, in a letter sent by him to Philippe Maria Visconti, Duke of Milan, in June 1429. The Duke had requested Boulainvilliers to send him news of the 'marvellous Maid'; his report read:

> This Maid has a certain elegance. She has a virile bearing, speaks little, shows an admirable prudence in all her words. She has a pretty, woman's voice, eats little, drinks very little wine; she enjoys riding a horse and takes pleasure in fine arms and greatly likes the company of noble fighting men, detests numerous assemblies and meetings, readily sheds copious tears, has a cheerful face; she bears the weight and burden of armour incredibly well, to such a point that she has remained fully armed during six days and nights.

No authentic, contemporary portrait of Joan is known to exist, but speculation has been made by Johannic scholars and other writers as to what she actually looked like. The later, fifteenth-century manuscript of the poems of Charles, Duke of Orléans, contains a miniature of Joan in armour; the face has certain characteristic features known from her contemporaries' descriptions, and the artist may have worked from indications given by someone who had known her.

A more compelling representation of Joan's facial features can be seen in a sculpted head in bronze (now in the Musée Jeanne d'Arc in Orléans). The head is all that remains of a statue, formerly to be found in the now demolished church of Saint-Maurice. There is a tradition that when Joan entered Orléans in triumph after the siege was raised a sculptor modelled the head of his statue of St Maurice from Joan herself.

Commenting on this possible likeness to Joan, the eminent English author and Johannic scholar W.S. Scott, in his book *Jeanne d'Arc, Her Life, Her Death, and the Myth*, wrote:

> It is unquestionably the head of a girl of nineteen or so; she wears a helmet of the period, and has the slightly prominent eyes which some believe to have been characteristic of the Maid. The face has a spiritual beauty which is most remarkable—a loveliness of expression which quite transcends that of mere physical beauty. Taking these points into consideration, it is difficult not to believe that in this fragment we have a true representation of the heroine.

George Bernard Shaw similarly expressed his conviction about the head in the preface to his play *Saint Joan*:

> A sculptor of her time in Orléans made a statue of a helmeted young woman with a face that is unique in art in point of being not an ideal

face but a portrait, and yet so uncommon as to be unlike any real woman one has ever seen. It is surmised that Joan served unconsciously as the sculptor's model. There is no proof of this; but these extraordinarily spaced eyes raise so powerfully the question 'If this woman be not Joan, who is she?' that I dispense with further evidence, and challenge those who disagree with me to prove a negative.

Accompanied by some of the dignitaries of the Dauphin's court, including Raoul de Gaucourt and the Archbishop of Reims, Joan journeyed to Blois, arriving on 24 April, to find the army and the supplies assembled, ready to march on Orléans to raise the siege.

At Blois, Joan met the leading captains of the army for the first time, amongst whom were the Marshal of France, Jean de Boussac, the Admiral of France, Louis de Coulant, and Gilles de Laval, Baron of Rais (known to history as Gilles de Rais, the later infamous 'Bluebeard'). She also met the Gascon, Etienne de Vignolles, known for his violent temperament as 'La Hire'. A hardened and experienced soldier of fortune, he was notorious, even by the military standards of the day, as the worst blasphemer in the army; he became one of Joan's greatest supporters and she even managed to convert him by persuading him to swear only by his baton, his staff of office.

Believing that a strong morality was essential for success in battle, Joan now set about a thorough reorganization of the moral standards of the whole army—which must have been something of a miracle, considering the nature of armies in those days. At first she was most unpopular, but in a very short time she was successful in banishing the camp followers, would allow no blaspheming or gambling, and insisted on regular observance of the religious practices, which she herself scrupulously followed throughout her mission. Soon all ranks, from the captains to the ordinary foot-soldiers, accepted everything she asked of them, and the initial resentment moved very quickly from opposition to veneration of her words and actions.

The army left Blois on 27 April, to set out for Orléans 'by the Sologne way', that is, on the opposite bank of the Loire from Orléans. There is a wonderful eyewitness account of the departure by Jean

Pasquerel, in which he describes the magnificent sight of Joan bearing her standard and riding at the head of the army, now some seven thousand strong, while he and the clergy led the entire procession, with everyone singing the *Veni Creator Spiritus*.

4   Orléans

The siege of Orléans has been the subject of countless, very detailed studies, the first being a contemporary account, which has survived to the present day: the Journal du Siège d'Orléans, a day-to-day account of the latter part of the siege and its deliverance.

That the city had been besieged at all was considered to be against all the rules of chivalric conduct, because in medieval warfare it was accepted practice that no place should be attacked unless its feudal lord was there to defend it, and Charles, Duke of Orléans, was at that time a prisoner in England.

The English army, under the leadership of Thomas Montague, Earl of Salisbury, whose previous victories in the area had no doubt led him to believe that Orléans would be his next prize, marched on the city on 12 October 1428.

However, at the start of the siege, the inhabitants from the surrounding areas and the citizens of the city demolished the suburbs, in order that the English would be without shelter, and withdrew into the town itself, thereby swelling the population to some 50,000 persons.

The English then set about strengthening the bastilles and boulevards (earthworks) placed at intervals outside the city; some of these were close together, others more widely spaced, which meant that the city was never entirely surrounded. The 4000 soldiers under Salisbury were not at sufficient strength to attack and take the city, but satisfied themselves by taking the fortified stone structure known as the Tourelles on the left bank of the Loire, at the entrance to the single bridge leading into the city.

Leaving the Tourelles under the command of Sir William Glasdale and 500 men, the main army withdrew for the time being to the towns in the vicinity that they had taken earlier.

Salisbury had been killed in battle shortly after the start of the siege, and at the beginning of December, when further English forces arrived, now under the joint leadership of John Talbot, Earl of Shrewsbury, and William de la Pole, Earl of Suffolk, there began a regular bombardment of the city. Records, however, state that this had little effect, and a situation more or less of stalemate existed, with forays on both sides from time to time.

By the time Joan and the French army marched on the city it was still heavily besieged and undergoing the greatest deprivation, with the population reduced to a state of near starvation. Therefore, when the news arrived that the famous *Pucelle* was riding towards the city with the army and the much needed provisions, there was great excitement amongst the inhabitants.

Of the many eyewitness accounts of Joan's arrival on Friday, 29 April, that of Jean, Count of Dunois, Bastard of Orléans, is one of the most vivid. He was the bastard son of Duke Louis of Orléans, who had been assassinated on the orders of John the Fearless, Duke of Burgundy, an act which led to the longstanding Armagnac-Burgundian feud. As half-brother to the imprisoned Charles, Jean had taken over the role of feudal lord of the city.

From their first meeting on the heights overlooking Orléans, the Bastard became Joan's most faithful friend and devoted companion-at-arms, whose loyalty towards her remained constant to the end. He would even lead a bold, but unsuccessful, attempt to free her, following her betrayal and capture at Compiègne.

At their first meeting, however, Joan, impatient as always to confront the enemy, was far from pleased when she learned that Dunois, being of the opinion that there were insufficient soldiers to defend and conduct the supplies into the city, had decided to delay any attack; also the direction of the current of the Loire and the direction of the wind made it impossible to cross the river.

'Are you the Bastard of Orléans?' were Joan's first words. 'I am,' he replied, 'and I rejoice that you are here.' 'Was it you who advised me to come here, on this side of the river, instead of going straight to where the English are?' was Joan's testy reply. When Dunois tried to explain how he and the other captains had decided in council to do what they thought best, Joan replied, 'In God's name, the Lord's counsel is better and wiser than yours. You thought to deceive me, but it is you who have deceived yourselves, for I am bringing you better help than you have ever had from any soldier or any city; it is succour from the King of Heaven, which does not come for love of me, but from God himself who, on the request of St Louis and St Charlemagne, has taken pity on the town of Orléans.'

'At this moment,' continued Dunois, 'the wind changed and became favourable. Sails were raised and the boats passed the church of Saint-Loup without interference from the English. From that moment I had great hopes of her, greater than before. I then implored her to cross the river and enter into the town, where she was most eagerly awaited.'

After some hesitation about leaving the main body of the army, Joan was assured that it would follow a route further to the west, towards Blois, from where it would be better positioned to return for the future attack on the city. Then, bearing her standard, Joan made the crossing, accompanied by Dunois, La Hire and the other captains.

At 8 o'clock that evening, Joan made a triumphal entry into the city, to a tumultuous reception by the inhabitants and, it is recorded, in a mighty thunderstorm, which, in adding its voice to that of the population, seemed to bestow a heavenly blessing on the events taking place below.

Riding on a white charger and 'armed at all points', with Dunois on her left, 'very richly armed and mounted', as the Journal du Siège recorded, Joan's standard was carried before her. Accompanied by a large retinue of armed knights and men-at-arms, they were joined by some of the burgesses of Orléans as the entire procession made its way through the streets.

The Journal also states at this point that the great throng of people were 'making such rejoicing as if they had seen God descend in their midst ... they felt themselves already comforted and as if no longer besieged, by the divine virtue ... in this simple maid, who looked upon them right affectionately, whether men, women or children.'

Such was the press of people, many bearing torches, that as the crowd surged forward Joan's standard caught fire. But, much to the admiration of the crowd, she deftly struck the spurs into her horse and, turning him on the standard, quickly extinguished the flames.

The entire company then made its way to the house of Jacques Boucher, the Treasurer of Orléans, where Joan would be lodged in the following days, and where, much to her joy, she was joined by her brothers, Jean and Pierre, who had come to fight alongside her. Pierre would be captured with Joan at Compiègne and imprisoned for a number of years thereafter, until he was able to raise his ransom.

On Saturday, 30 April, Joan was very angry and frustrated, as the captains had decided that no action was possible until the main army returned. Later that day she had to content herself by shouting across to the English from one of the fortifications outside the city, that 'in God's name' they should withdraw or she would have to drive them out, but they only replied with insults. She tried again, calling to the commander in the Tourelles, Sir William Glasdale, to 'yield to God's command', but their reply was to call her 'cowgirl' and loudly cry that, if they could lay hands on her, they would have her burned. Already, the more superstitious among the enemy seem to have made up their minds that Joan was using witchcraft against them—a charge which her judges would later bring against her at her trial.

On Sunday, 1 May, Dunois and a small party left to bring the army back from its encampment at Blois. Joan and a number of soldiers accompanied them for some distance as protection. Much to their surprise, the English made no attempt to intercept them, and this was also the case when they returned to the city; as one record stated, 'not an Englishman stirred'. In fact, from the time of Joan's appearance, there was an ever-increasing reluctance by the enemy to make any really decisive moves; her reputation for possessing supernatural powers created a real fear of her, particularly among the lower ranks.

During that day, Joan and her retinue rode again through the streets of Orléans, following an episode when, it is recorded, the citizens almost broke down the door where she was lodged, so anxious were they to see her again. As she went through the streets, the very sight of her, sitting her horse 'with such ease and grace', made the people marvel and say that she had the air of 'a man-at-arms who had followed the wars since youth'.

On Monday, 2 May, Joan rode outside the city walls to reconnoitre the enemy positions, which were found to be of formidable strength. She later went to the church of Sainte-Croix in the city, to offer prayers for the success of her mission.

A procession to honour Joan was conducted throughout the city, on Tuesday, 3 May, with people along the route imploring her to quickly deliver them from the siege. Later, money and gifts were made to her and her companions.

Wednesday, 4 May, saw the first crucial battle for the raising of the siege. In the morning, Dunois returned with the reinforcements and Joan rode out to meet him, eagerly anticipating an early battle, but Dunois appeared reluctant to take any action. Later, after taking a meal together, he told Joan that he had it on good authority that Sir John Fastolf was approaching Orléans with reinforcements for the English army. Joan, aroused at this news and becoming increasingly frustrated by Dunois' inactivity, was reported by her squire, d'Aulon, to have said to Dunois, 'Bastard, Bastard, in God's name I command thee that when thou knowest Fastolf is come, make it known to me; for if he gets through without my knowing, I swear I will have thy head taken off!' Dunois apparently answered that he did not for one moment doubt it!

After this, with everyone fatigued, Joan, with her page, Louis de Coutes, and d'Aulon went to her chambers to rest, Joan on one bed with her hostess, as was her custom. As d'Aulon recounted, he was about to fall asleep, when Joan suddenly let out a cry that her Voices had told her to go out against the English, but that she was uncertain as to whether they meant against the fortifications or against Fastolf's approaching army. As d'Aulon quickly dressed Joan in her armour, some confusion then occurred when, as de Coutes related, at Joan's sudden awakening she turned on him exclaiming, '*Ah, sanglant garçon* (bloody boy), you did not tell me that the blood of France was being spilt!' Urging him to fetch her horse, she rushed downstairs, forgetting her standard, which de Coutes had to pass to her through a window, as she rode off towards her first military encounter.

Why Joan had not been informed of this proposed attack, which was directed against the Bastille Saint-Loup, is difficult to understand. Obviously, the seasoned captains were used to making all the crucial decisions regarding combat tactics; but this was not the only time when Joan would be excluded from their councils-of-war. It is a matter of record that she had often to fight their decisions and remind them of the divine source at work behind all her actions in battle. From the time of Agincourt in 1415, the greatest French commanders had failed to defeat the English enemy, and it was not until Joan's emergence in this year of 1429 that the tide began to turn in France's favour; perhaps it was the case that these men did not yet realize Joan's true significance.

It is not known why the decision was made to attack Saint-Loup; it was not the most important nor the most strategically placed fort but, as Joan rode in the direction of the fighting, she heard the sounds of a battle in full swing. Meeting some of the soldiers, who were carrying their dead and wounded, Joan was horrified to learn that the French were in retreat and that some 1500 of them had been driven back by only 400 of the English holding the fort, following three hours of fierce fighting.

When Joan arrived at the scene, a great cheer went up from the soldiers. Fresh troops arrived with siege weapons and scaling ladders. The English archers began to rain down their arrows on the French attackers, but in a very short time the fort was taken and the enemy either killed or taken prisoner. There were very few French losses, but Joan was distraught at the bloodshed involved on both sides, and wept for those who had died without confession.

In the events that took place on that day, 4 May, it can be seen that the battle was all but lost, until Joan's appearance inspired the soldiers to make their further, successful assault. It was due to her actual presence at the scene of action that the day was won.

There has been much debate about Joan's prowess as a military leader and strategist, and many great military figures, including Napoleon, have regarded her as a genius in these fields; others have been equally convinced that she was merely a mascot, a symbol dreamt up by the French in a last desperate attempt to inject some heart into a previously demoralized and defeated army. But neither opinion is satisfactory in explaining the miraculous effect she had on those around her, whether they were hardened military leaders, the roughest of soldiery or, indeed, all who came within her orbit. It was Joan's *actual presence* which lifted broken spirits and inspired hope and courage in all.

What was the real nature of the tremendous effect she had on all with whom she came into contact? Not simply Joan, the shining figure in her white armour—an extraordinary and singular phenomenon in itself—nor her prowess as a brilliant military leader, which was, certainly at this point, virtually untried.

Even at her first appearance in Orléans, the populace reacted towards her, as the Journal recorded, 'as if they had seen God descend in their midst'. What was felt and experienced in human souls was the tremendous strength and energy of the Christ Impulse, the compelling Christ Force, which radiated from her with such powerful effect.

What Rudolf Steiner speaks of as 'Christ's real and visibly active power' was here manifest in European history, which, as he tells us, has been guided by the Christ Impulse since the Mystery of Golgotha. The Christ Impulse was present in the soul of Joan of Arc, 'inspiring her to act as its human shell on the battlefields of France'.

The deed of Joan of Arc at the beginning of the Consciousness Soul age was, as Rudolf Steiner explained, of momentous significance:

> ... not the human mind nor the talents of military leaders were decisive factors in changing the map of Europe so magnificently, but rather the Christ Impulse working itself into the subconscious of the Maid of Orléans and inspiring her to radiate its presence in all of history.

Pasquerel testified that 4 May was the eve of Ascension Day, and Joan confessed herself to him and received the Eucharist. She told him to exhort the soldiers to confess also, and give thanks for the victory; otherwise she would not stay with them. Also, that women of ill-repute were not to be allowed to follow the army, 'for it was for these sins that God allowed the war to be lost'.

On the feast day of the Ascension, Joan decided that she would not fight, out of respect for the holiness of the day. But she told Pasquerel that, within five days, the siege would be lifted and the English gone.

As attested by Louis de Coutes, Joan ate very little on the days of battle and so, following her usual frugal meal of bread and watered wine, she retired for the night. Thus, the first day of victory ended.

On Thursday, 5 May, Joan dictated her third letter to the English commanders. She had sent the first letter while undergoing her examination at Poitiers; the time of the second is not known, but each letter contained a similar ultimatum and a warning:

> You, Englishmen, who have no right in the Kingdom of France, the King of Heaven commands you by me, Joan the Maid, to leave

your forts and return to your own country. If you do not do so, I shall make you such a *hahay* that it will live in perpetual memory. I write this to you for the third and last time, and I shall not write again.

Signed: *Jhesus Maria*

Joan the Maid

The letter was tied to an arrow, which an archer shot into the Tourelles, shouting, 'Read, here is news!,' to which the English replied, 'Here is news from the Armagnac whore!' Pasquerel said that Joan then 'began to sigh and weep copious tears, invoking the King of Heaven to her aid. But later she was comforted, as she had news of her Lord.' Presumably her Heavenly Counsel had spoken and reassured her that, even though the English had repulsed her ultimatum, she had, nevertheless, done everything possible by her attempt.

On Friday, 6 May, it was decided to attack the Bastille Saint-Jean-le-Blanc on the south side of the river. The assault was led by Joan and La Hire, who crossed in two boats with their horses, the soldiers crossing on foot through the shallows. Upon arriving at the opposite bank it was discovered that the enemy, on seeing their approach, had retreated to the stronger position of the Bastille des Augustins.

Having decided to return in the direction of the city, the French found themselves attacked from the rear by the English streaming out from the Augustins. Joan, undeterred, ordered that they would turn and fight, which they successfully accomplished, killing and capturing many of the enemy, and the Bastille was finally taken. The remaining English again retreated, this time to the Tourelles, the very strongly fortified position at the far end of the only bridge leading into the city.

With a sense of triumph, Joan returned to her lodgings, suffering from exhaustion and, having stepped on a calthrop—a spiked metal ball—which had pierced her foot during the battle, she decided against her usual Friday fast and took a meal.

Later that evening, the French captains again met without Joan, and decided against any attack on the following day, fearing their troops were under strength for an assault on the Tourelles. When news of their decision reached Joan, she was furious to learn that they had again taken a decision without her. Confronting them, she said, 'You have been with your counsel, and I have been with mine, and believe me the Counsel of God will triumph, while yours will fail.'

To Pasquerel, she said, 'Rise tomorrow, even earlier than you did today, and stay near me, for I shall have yet greater deeds to do, and blood will flow from my body above my breast.'

Saturday, 7 May, saw the crucial attack on the Tourelles. This fortification had been built over the last of the 19 spans supporting the only bridge over the Loire, which led into the city, and consisted of two flanking towers and a drawbridge separating it from the bank of the river. It was further protected by a boulevard thrown up by the English earlier in the siege. A formidable stronghold, it was well defended by some 600–800 men (figures vary), and was under the command of Sir William Glasdale.

Very early that morning, Joan and the army heard Pasquerel say Mass, after which they crossed the river to the Augustins to meet with the leading French captains, prominent amongst whom were Dunois and La Hire. Again there was doubt about the proposed attack on the Tourelles, but Joan managed to convince them, roundly swearing that, 'By Saint-Martin, I will take it today, and re-enter the city over this bridge.'

The battle, which began around 7 o'clock in the morning, would last until sunset. The French simultaneously attacked from three sides, but the English were heavily armed with a variety of weaponry, from heavy cannon to axes and lances, and resisted strongly, causing many casualties among the French.

Although they attacked again and again, it was not until late morning that the French were able to get close enough to the walls to place their scaling ladders. Joan was among the first to do so, and it was then that she received the wound which she had predicted; an arrow entered above her left breast, between her neck and shoulder, penetrating to a depth of six inches.

Seeing that Joan was wounded, some of the English soldiers let themselves down from the walls to try to reach her, but a French knight quickly dismounted and gave her his horse, and she was led away from the action. Safe from danger, she pulled the arrow out herself.

Pasquerel, who was at her side, recalled:

> ...when she felt that she was wounded, she was frightened and wept... And when some soldiers saw her wounded, they wanted to lay a charm on her, but she refused it, saying, 'I would rather die than do a thing which I know to be a sin; I know well that I must die one day, but I know not when, nor in what manner, nor on what day; but if my wound may be healed without sin, I shall be glad enough to be cured.' Olive oil and lard were then applied to the wound. After the dressing, she confessed herself to me, weeping and lamenting. Then she returned in all haste to the attack.

When Joan returned to the scene of battle, she found that the English, who doubtless thought that she was seriously wounded and out of the fighting, and confident they had the upper hand, began to stream out of the Tourelles and onto the drawbridge between the main fort and the outer defences.

On seeing Glasdale standing on the drawbridge at the head of his men, Joan called to him, 'Glasdale! Glasdale! Yield, yield to the King of Heaven! You have called me harlot, but I have great pity for your soul and for your men's souls.'

At this point, the French were filling a barge with wood and sulphur, which they then towed under the drawbridge and set on fire. The main body of the English, fearing they would be cut off, withdrew into the main fort, while Glasdale and other knights covered their retreat. But suddenly the charred drawbridge collapsed and Glasdale and his men fell into the river, their heavy armour preventing them from being able to save themselves, and all were drowned.

Upon seeing this, Pasquerel stated that 'Joan, moved to pity, began to weep bitterly for the soul of Glasdale and of the rest.'

Accounts vary as to the following events, but the fierce fighting continued throughout the day. In the evening, Dunois decided there was no hope of victory and began to make plans for a retreat into the city, but Joan asked him to wait a little while longer. Mounting her horse, she rode off into a vineyard nearby to be alone; after some minutes spent in prayer she returned and, according to Dunois' account, seized her standard and began to rally the troops. As they advanced, the English, upon seeing the unexpected sight of the French surging towards them, 'trembled with terror' as Dunois recalled. Later reports even circulated to the effect that, in their great alarm, the English had actually observed the Archangel Michael and St Aignan, the patron saint of Orléans, riding on horseback in mid-air to the aid of the French!

Whatever the truth regarding this phenomenon, there was certainly great panic and disarray among the English ranks, thus enabling the French to make a final, fierce assault, capturing the Tourelles with great loss of life to those within. The day had seen what proved to be the last battle for the raising of the siege.

Joan and the army then crossed back into the city—over the bridge, as she had foretold; she had her wound dressed and took her only meal of that day, consisting of 'four or five toasts soaked in well-watered wine'.

Joan's squire, Jean d'Aulon, in his later testimony for the Rehabilitation, recalled that, following the victory, the citizens of Orléans

> ... made great rejoicing and praised Our Lord for this great victory which He had given them; and right was it that they should do so, for it is said that this assault ... was so greatly fought in both attack and defence, that it was one of the greatest feats of arms that there had been for a long time ... And the clergy and people of Orléans sang devoutly *Te deum laudamus* and caused all the bells of the city to be pealed, most humbly thanking Our Lord for that glorious divine consolation. And made great joy on all sides, giving marvellous praises to their valiant defenders, and above all to Joan the Maid.

At dawn on Sunday, 8 May, Joan was informed that the English had left their remaining siege positions and had formed up ready for battle. She had herself armed and the French army also lined up in attack formation. Each side faced their enemy for the space of an hour, neither making any move to attack, although many of the French were impatient to do so, desiring to capitalize on their victory of the previous day. However, Joan reminded them that this was a holy day, when it was not permissible to fight, unless attacked first, and during the hour that followed, she ordered a portable altar to be set up on the battlefield, and two Masses were said to the entire French army.

After the ceremony, Joan asked whether the enemy had their backs or their faces towards them. On hearing that their backs were turned and the English were in retreat, Joan said, 'Let them go; it is not the Lord's pleasure that we should fight them today; you will get them another time.'

The English were not allowed to escape entirely peacefully, as some of the French were unable to restrain themselves, and made a number of assaults on the English rear, capturing not only lighter weaponry, but also some heavy cannon and bombards.

Why the English retreated at this juncture is something of a mystery. According to accounts, they were still well-provisioned and armed, and reinforcements were expected at any time. Perhaps the events of the previous day had left them so demoralized that it was thought better strategy to withdraw to some of the fortified towns they had captured earlier in the area, where they could regroup and work out new plans for future combat.

At any rate, depart they did, after seven months of siege, which Joan had succeeded in raising in ten days—thus was fulfilled the first part of her mission.

★ ★ ★

Joyous celebrations continued in Orléans, with processions and services of thanksgiving in the churches. The gratitude of the citizens never waned, and they would go in great numbers to Paris in 1455 with Joan's mother, when she presented her petition in the cathedral of Notre Dame for Joan's rehabilitation.

The date of the city's deliverance on 8 May was established as a feast day, and has continued annually to the present time, even surviving the chaotic period of the French Revolution. Each year, ceremonies and parades are held, culminating in a service in the cathedral of Sainte-Croix, with a panegyric to Joan being read out to the people of the city by an invited dignitary.

★ ★ ★

It was not only in Orléans, nor indeed only in France, that Joan's increasing fame was celebrated. Throughout Europe, ambassadors to France were writing to their royal and aristocratic heads of state in Italy, Germany and elsewhere, in answer to requests to send news of the 'marvellous Maid'. Their letters and journals have survived to testify to the tremendous interest aroused by Joan's appearance.

Alain Chartier, one of the great poets of the time, ended his letter to a foreign prince:

> Here is she who seems not to issue from any place on earth, but rather sent by Heaven to sustain with head and shoulders a France fallen to the ground. O astonishing virgin! worthy of all fame, of all praise, worthy of all the divine honours! Thou art the honour of the reign, thou art the light of the lily, thou art the splendour, the glory, not only of Gaul but of all Christians.

Another of France's great writers, the poetess Christine de Pisan, was the first to elevate Joan in verse. As the first woman in France to enjoy a literary career, she had written widely in her prose and poetic works on love, history and politics. Although she had retired to a nunnery in 1418, upon the entry of the English into Paris, and had written nothing thereafter, she had obviously retained a deep interest in the outside world, and had remained aware of the dire political situation in France. Now, at the age of 66, she took up her pen again and, by July 1429, in what was possibly her last work (she died in 1431 and never met Joan), she composed her *Stances*, which show her joy at the upturn in the fortunes of France:

> Year fourteen hundred and twenty-nine
> Once more the sun began to shine,
> And with it all good times began
> As long they had not done.
> I lived and hoped through those long years
> As so did many a one,
> No longer do I need to hope
> For my longed-for wish is come.
>
> (An imperfect translation, but it gives the sense of the poetess's lines.)

Christine's devout faith and spiritual insight inspired her to a recognition of the deeper significance of Joan's role, when she wrote:

> You, Joan, born at the right time
> Praised be He who created you!

Virgin ordained by God
To whom the Holy Spirit rayed forth
His great grace...

★ ★ ★

As for the English, two royal mandates would later be issued against army deserters, who had apparently fled, 'terrified by the Maid's enchantments'. From the start, the English had made up their minds that Joan was a witch—how else could she have achieved such success against them? This would be one of the charges the judges would lay against her at her trial. Even after her death, the English view of Joan still doggedly persisted, as in the belief expressed in a letter written by the Duke of Bedford to the young King Henry VI, in which he spoke of her as 'a disciple and lyme of the Feende, called the Pucelle'.

5　The Loire Campaign

Joan and her retinue lost no time in leaving Orléans, which they did on 9 or 10 May. She was anxious to undertake the next stage of her mission: to have the Dauphin crowned at Reims. As she would repeatedly stress, until Charles was made king his position was less than secure, but with his consecration the strength of the English would decline and would no longer be a threat to the kingdom of France.

With this belief Joan rode off to Tours where Charles had taken up residence; here, and some days later at Loches, where the court then moved, Joan began to battle for further, positive action to be taken to clear the way north in order for the coronation to take place.

Dunois' account of Joan's meeting with Charles stated that Joan fell on her knees before him and embraced his legs, saying, 'Noble Dauphin, do not spend so much time in council, but come with me as quickly as possible to Reims to receive your crown.'

There then followed some hesitation by Charles who was, as usual, allowing himself to be influenced by dissenting factions within his court, led by La Trémoille.

One of those present then asked Joan how she could be so certain that they could have confidence in her and was it her Counsel that told her to act. Charles also asked her to explain her motivation, which she said she would willingly do, and, as Dunois stated:

> She said her voices had become more pressing and that she had retired apart to pray to God, complaining to Him that those to whom she spoke would not believe her. And when she had prayed, she heard a voice which said, 'Go, Daughter of God, go, and I will help you.' And when she heard this voice she felt a great joy and wished she could always be in this happy state. And what is more, when she thus repeated to us the words of her voices, she was seized with a marvellous rapture and raised her eyes to heaven.

Joan's inspired words seemed to have won the argument, but some still questioned whether it would not be better to make the next offensive in Normandy, with the eventual hope that Paris might be taken. But Joan remained firm that her Voices had told her that Reims was the most pressing objective, and she eventually won them over to her plan.

Meanwhile, as news of Joan's victory at Orléans spread far and wide, the French army began to grow rapidly in strength and numbers, with many influential knights allying themselves to the Dauphin's cause. Charles gave the command of the royal army to the Duke of Alençon, for what was to be the Loire campaign, the objective of which would be to force the English out of the Loire region and further north, to give the rear of the army protection on its march towards Reims. It was decided to begin the offensive by making an attack on the fortified town of Jargeau, to where the remnants of the English army had retreated from Orléans under the Earl of Suffolk, who was also making plans for reinforcements to be assembled under Sir John Fastolf.

Riding around the area, Joan was next at Selles-en-Berri for some days, where she met a young knight, Guy de Laval, who with his brother André had come to join the army. The Lavals were grandsons of the Constable of France, the famous Bertrand du Guesclin. Possessing all the ardour of youth and obviously excited at the prospect of the coming conflict, Guy was enthralled at his first sight of Joan. In a letter to his mother he wrote:

> I saw the Maid mount her great black charger, armed entirely *en blanc* but for her head, and to see and hear her, she seemed like a being all divine.

He dined with Joan and was impressed by her confident assertion when she told him that he would soon be drinking wine in Paris.

Guy saw her departure from Selles on Wednesday, 8 June, and in his letter wrote of how Joan's charger reared up and would not let her mount, but she instructed that he be led to the cross in front of the church, whereupon he became calm and she was easily able to mount him. As the party began to set off, Guy describes Joan in her white armour, her head bare, and holding a little axe. She was accompanied by one of her brothers—no doubt Pierre, who had arrived in Selles some days before. Joan called to her page to unfurl her standard and the party rode off towards Romorantin where the Loire campaign was to begin.

The Loire Campaign

Joan next headed for Orléans, where the army was being regrouped. At this point Alençon had under his command 600 knights and 2000 soldiers, a figure which was doubled when the Bastard and other captains joined him with their forces.

The most vivid account of the campaign in the Loire we owe to Alençon, which was given by him in his Rehabilitation testimony. He speaks of the time when Joan had stayed with him and his wife at their home, just after the siege of Orléans was lifted. His wife, Jeanne, the daughter of the imprisoned Charles, Duke of Orléans, said she was much alarmed at the prospect of Alençon going off to fight again; he had only just finished paying off his ransom after being taken prisoner at the battle of Verneuil in 1424. Joan reassured her that she would bring him safely back 'and in such state or better than he now is'.

From Orléans Joan rode to Jargeau on Saturday, 11 June, to meet up with Alençon. Again she found disputes among the captains as to how best to attack the town, but Joan convinced them, exhorting them, as Alençon said, not to be afraid, 'for God was guiding them, and had she not been so certain, she would be better keeping her sheep rather than placing herself in peril'.

The French first encountered the English forces in the suburbs of the town, and were at first driven back, but Joan seized her standard and urged them forward, driving the enemy back into the town. As at Orléans, Joan then requested the English commanders to surrender, but again her request was refused.

The next morning Joan decided to take the town by storm. Alençon was somewhat doubtful about what he feared was a premature attempt, but Joan convinced him, saying, 'Forward, gentle Duke, to the attack; doubt not, the time is come when it pleases God; act and God will act.'

As the battle got under way, both sides used their gunpowder weaponry, which they appeared to have in abundance. As a fortified town, Jargeau would be difficult to capture, but the French continued to batter the fortifications, finally bringing down one of the main towers. Suffolk was sufficiently alarmed by the continuous assault that he tried to negotiate a kind of surrender, an offer he apparently made to La Hire without the knowledge of Joan or Alençon. This was refused, as it was realized that it was Suffolk's intention to stay put and wait for reinforcements. Joan did, however, offer to let both the English and any townspeople leave without harm, but the offer was declined.

During the continuing bombardment by both sides, Alençon testified that Joan told him to move away from the spot where he was standing, indicating a 'machine' on the town walls which would kill him if he stayed where he was. Alençon quickly moved, and a little later on that very spot where he had been standing 'the Lord de Lude, who was passing by, was killed'. Alençon spoke of his fear, and relief at this incident, adding that he marvelled at Joan's prophecy.

Joan next decided on an assault on the town walls and led the attack, carrying her standard. Fierce fighting ensued, which lasted for some hours without any real progress being made, as the English constantly forced them back. In an attempt to scale the walls, Joan began to climb a ladder, still bearing her standard, when a missile tore into it and, at the same time, she was struck on the head with a stone which pierced her helmet, knocking her into the dry moat below. Undaunted, Joan quickly recovered her feet and shouted to those around her, 'Friends, Friends, up, up! Our Lord has condemned the English! Have courage, in this hour they are ours!'

Emboldened by Joan's words, the French soldiers made an even more vigorous attack and, within a short time, the town was taken. French losses were not recorded, but those of the English were heavy and, although some fled, many were captured, among them the Earl of Suffolk. Unknown to Joan, the majority of those taken prisoner were slaughtered by the French soldiers, as was customary in those days, unless a ransom could be had, which was only in the case of those of high rank.

When Joan found out about the killings, she was filled with anguish for the dead and dying of both sides. Victory for her was always a bitter one, and as her page, Louis de Coutes said:

> Joan was very greatly distressed by the slaughter. Once when a Frenchman was bringing us some English prisoners, he knocked one of them on the head and left him for dead. When Joan saw this she dismounted and received the Englishman's confession, raising his head and comforting him as much as she could.

From Jargeau, Joan and the French captains left for Orléans to celebrate the victory but, during their first night there, Joan lost no time in reminding Alençon that it was vital they should move against the towns of Meung-sur-Loire and Beaugency, which were still occupied by the English forces.

On Wednesday, 15 June, the French army marched the short distance from Orléans to Meung, where it was discovered that the only obstacle confronting them was a fortified bridge outside the town which, notwithstanding a brave defence by the English, quickly fell to them, and the town was taken without further fighting. The French army then moved off in the direction of Beaugency.

It was at this point that the French were joined by Arthur de Richemont, Constable of France, leading a strong force of men-at-arms. His arrival was greeted with some apprehension by Joan and Alençon, because of his past reputation as an ally of Burgundy and England, an alliance which he had broken in 1424 when he was involved in a dispute with the English who had refused him an important command. He then sought to return to the Armagnac side and, because of his renowned military prowess, the Dauphin—no doubt pleased that his enemy had lost a valuable ally—conferred on him the highest military office, that of Constable, which carried the command of all the French forces. However, because de Richemont was at odds with certain influential factions within the French court, Charles subsequently deprived him of his status. Even so, he was apparently a powerful enough figure to retain a large force of his own.

Joan and Alençon knew of de Richemont's disgrace and were suspicious of his intentions, and when he arrived at Beaugency there was some rather cautious dialogue between them, as they tried to discover his motives. As their discussions were taking place, the news arrived that Sir John Fastolf was heading towards them with an estimated 4000–5000 men, and the decision was taken—fortunately, as it turned out—to accept the offer of de Richemont's aid without further hesitation.

Fastolf arrived on the scene while the French were making their first attack on the town. Both sides then began to draw up in battle formation but, surprisingly, neither side made any attempt to attack, but finally the English sent two heralds to suggest that the French should be the ones to make the first move; Joan replied that, as the hour was late, the English should return to their camp, adding, 'At the pleasure of God and Our Lady, we will take a look at one another tomorrow.'

Following Joan's message, Fastolf and his captains left—apparently, as she had suggested, for the night; but, when morning came, it was discovered that the entire English army had departed the scene, and it was assumed that, upon learning of de Richemont's arrival, Fastolf had become unnerved at the prospect of having to face a considerably enlarged and strengthened French side.

The assault on Beaugency was intensified, and continual bombardment of the fortifications led the English leaders to negotiate a surrender of the town. In return, they asked for safe passage to withdraw and gave their promise not to fight against the French for the next ten days. Alençon agreed to their terms and they departed during the night of 17 June. Joan was no doubt very satisfied that further bloodshed had been avoided, as this was always her most earnest hope. As he retreated north, Fastolf made a brief, abortive attack on Meung, but was quickly defeated by the arrival of a French contingent from the captured Beaugency.

As the English army retreated north, hoping to reach the strongly fortified town of Janville, Joan turned to Alençon, saying, 'Have you good spurs?' Those present interpreted her words to mean that they were about to turn their backs on the enemy, but Joan answered that they would have need of good spurs to chase after them. She knew that, until the Loire was entirely free, there would be no clear route to Reims.

Again, doubts were raised among the French captains, but Joan confidently asserted: 'In God's name, we must fight them! If they were hanging from the clouds we should get them! My Counsel has told me that they are ours, and the noble Dauphin shall have greater victory than he has ever had.'

The English army, having re-formed under Fastolf and Talbot, were now some 5000 strong. At first unaware of the pursuit by the French, they reached the area known as Patay, a large plain with woods and tall hedgerows. When it was realized by their rearguard that the French were rapidly approaching, Fastolf made the decision to stand and fight. Ordering the main body of the army to hide in the woods, he took his mounted archers, some 500 strong, towards an area where he thought the French would have to pass, and positioned them in the usual defensive formation adopted by the English—a formation which had won them victories, notably at Agincourt. Fastolf's strategy was that the archers would hold off the English long enough for him to bring up the main army behind the French in a surprise attack.

As the French approached, headed by La Hire and his cavalry, they were followed by the main army, some 6000 strong, and commanded by the Constable, Alençon and the Bastard. The French realized they had lost the desired element of surprise, and arrived on the plain to find an apparently deserted scene.

Suddenly, an amazing incident occurred, which dramatically affected the action, when a stag ran out of the woods, straight into the body of archers. Alarmed, they let out a loud cry, which was heard by the French vanguard, who turned and rode back to inform the main army.

The English archers then fled into the depths of the wood where the main body of their army had hidden, an action which caused great confusion in the ranks, with the soldiers believing that a retreat was imminent. The entire army hastily began to take flight before Fastolf could order a defence. The French army quickly charged into the fleeing soldiers, and in less than an hour 2000 of the English had been killed, while the French casualties were few. In the melée, Fastolf managed to escape, but Talbot and other leaders were captured. The remnants of the English army managed a disorderly retreat north, where they hoped to find refuge in the English stronghold in Paris.

With the victory at Patay on Saturday, 18 June, thus ended the series of battles which later became known as the Week of Victories.

There has been much debate about Joan's role in the battle of Patay. Some have seen it as her greatest triumph, but as there is little mention of her on this day, others have doubted whether she took any heroic action, as in previous conflicts. But, in any case, inspired by her Counsel, hers was the decision to waste no time in the pursuit of the English forces. Had they escaped and had time to regroup, this could have greatly affected the later situation for the French—possibly resulting in defeat, but certainly in delay for Joan's much longed-for plans for Charles' coronation.

Constantly urged to act by her Counsel, Joan knew that time was short. Alençon testified that he had sometimes heard her say to the Dauphin, 'Use me well, for I shall last but a year.'

* * *

The high point of Joan's mission was undoubtedly reached with the sweeping victories of the Loire campaign; but the near future would see the marshalling of the ahrimanic and luciferic powers which, in concerted effort, and by acting through the treacheries and weaknesses of those around her, would try their utmost to destroy her and her mission.

For the moment, however, Rudolf Steiner's deeply spiritual explanation that, in Joan, 'the Christ Impulse entered her soul, enabling her to act as its human shell on the battlefields of France', still held true in this fierce struggle between the forces, both spiritual and earthly, locked in combat at this crucial period of European history.

Joan's involvement in war will always remain an enigma, unless a deeper insight is sought into her actions in this earlier part of her mission. Rudolf Steiner has shed light on her role and that of warlike deeds generally, when he explains how progress in certain aspects of human development could only be achieved by warlike means:

> Modern ideas now consider warlike deeds to be a relic of the past, but in the earlier history of Europe the most characteristic moral forces given to Christianity as a moral possession, a moral heritage, were valour or bravery—this is the chief virtue of the Europeans, particularly those of North and Central Europe; the whole of personal human force was exercised in order to actualize in the physical world what the human being intends from his innermost impulse. This was the origin of the impulse of chivalry. And bravery and valour produce definite moral effects in the evolution of humanity.

Although the chivalric ideal was now a thing of the past, its influence could still be felt in human souls, and the radiant figure of Joan in her white armour was able to evoke this ideal in the hearts of the fighting men she led into battle.

6   Reims

Joan had returned to Orléans, following the Loire campaign, where she constantly fretted at what she believed to be an unnecessary delay in setting out for the march to Reims and the much longed-for coronation. She was now at the head of an army some 12,000 strong, its dramatic increase in numbers occasioned by her recent victories; news of her successes at Orléans and in the Loire had spread like wildfire throughout the whole of France. Many who had previously hesitated to ally themselves with the Dauphin's cause—the knights, men-at-arms, and even ordinary citizens—had flocked in great numbers to join the army. Everyone believed that in this saintly girl they had found the saviour of their land.

As for the English and the Burgundians in their various strongholds along the proposed route to Reims, they were soon to dread the approach of Joan and her vast army.

On Friday, 24 June, Joan arrived with the army at Gien, where the Dauphin had taken up residence with his court, and she immediately began to entreat him to set out for Reims. Alençon fully supported her in this, but the Dauphin's Council, headed by his Chamberlain, Georges de la Trémoille, and Regnault de Chartres, Archbishop of Reims, were in direct opposition to her plans. They favoured an attempt at a diplomatic approach or awaiting further victories over the enemy before proceeding with the coronation plans.

These two powerful men were, from the start, Joan's opponents in her relations with the Dauphin, and would eventually become her most implacable enemies. La Trémoille, known because of his huge bulk as 'the Fat Councillor', was jealous of Joan's influence with the Dauphin. Throughout his life he had exhibited very ambitious and often devious political aspirations and had earlier served John the Fearless of Burgundy. He never entirely severed his connection, manoeuvring politically between Burgundian interests and those of the Dauphin. De Chartres had been made Archbishop of Reims by the Pope 20 years earlier, but had never in fact been to that city to take up his position there.

Whilst conflicting advice once again prevented Charles from arriving at a decision, both he and Joan had letters despatched to the citizens of the towns through which they would pass on the road to Reims. Charles' letters granted amnesty to all loyal Frenchmen and invited them to follow him to his anointing, while Joan, after reminding them of her past victories under the leadership of the King of Heaven, was also quick to inform them of what she would do to their lives and property if she and the Dauphin were not received in a peaceful manner.

By Monday, 27 June, action had still not been decided upon and, feeling even more frustrated, Joan left the town and encamped with the army, declaring, 'By my *martin*' (her baton, or staff of office—the only oath she allowed herself), 'I will lead the noble Dauphin and his company safely, and he will be crowned at Reims.'

Joan's resolute statement seems to have had an immediate and convincing effect upon the military captains, who then made clear to the Dauphin their determination to follow Joan, and he finally gave the orders to move.

On Wednesday, 29 June, the Dauphin, with his entire court, and with Joan leading the army, set out on the first stage of the journey to Reims, their north-eastern route taking them first to Auxerre, which they reached on Thursday, 30 June. The town had long been under Burgundian control, but faced with the huge army, the town's governors quickly negotiated terms of surrender and opened its gates after three days. Charles forgave all those in the town who had been involved with the enemy and no blood was shed.

The next place along the route was the strongly fortified town of Troyes, another longstanding Anglo-Burgundian bastion. Joan sent a letter ahead, addressed to the 'Very good and dear friends', the citizens of Troyes, advising them of the Dauphin's approach with the army, at the same time warning them of what would happen, should they fail to welcome Charles, who appended a guarantee of amnesty if the town were to surrender peacefully.

The town's officials, however, chose to ignore Joan's letter, and when the French army arrived outside the town on Tuesday, 5 July, it was to find the drawbridge and all the gates closed against them. Eventually, from what transpired to be only a small defending force, which made a brief foray outside the town, it would appear that, once again, the size of the French army acted as a deterrent to any further action.

For four days negotiations were carried out, with the Troyennes unwilling to submit, although Joan begged them to do so. Her reputation had, to some extent, preceded her, but it seems to have been influenced by their superstition regarding her supernatural powers, and the decision was taken to send a Franciscan friar to put some pertinent theological questions to her.

This mendicant friar, Brother Richard, had the somewhat dubious reputation of being able to predict the future, and had even foretold that the end of the world would take place in 1430. But his predictions had always turned out to be false, and he had been driven out of Paris some time before and would soon suffer the same exit from Troyes. His visit to Joan was the subject of an interrogation by the judges at her trial, in one of their determined attempts to prove that she had used witchcraft and sorcery to accomplish her mission. To this accusation, Joan would answer:

> The people of the town of Troyes sent him to me, saying that they feared that I was not a thing of God, and when he came towards me, he made signs of the cross and sprinkled holy water, but I said to him, 'Approach boldly, I shall not fly away.'

The friar, seeing that Joan remained rooted to the spot, quickly left to make a very disappointing report about his efforts at exorcism. Even so, he appears to have been much impressed by Joan, as he accompanied her to Reims, sometimes acting as her confessor, but no doubt revelling in the attention he enjoyed from his association with her.

Discussions next took place between the Dauphin and the army captains as to whether to lay siege to the town, or to bypass it and go directly on to Reims. But according to Dunois, Joan said to Charles, 'Noble Dauphin, order your people to go and besiege the city of Troyes and stay no longer in council for, in God's name, within three days I will take you into the city of Troyes by love or by force or by courage, and false Burgundy will stand amazed.'

Arrangements for the siege were quickly put in place, with Joan directing the operations, instructing the artillery to be set against the walls of the town, and supervising everything down to the last detail. This so impressed Dunois that he would recall, after more than 25 years, how she 'made admirable dispositions such as could not have been done better by the most experienced soldiers'.

Preparations continued throughout the night, and the townspeople awoke the following morning to witness the tremendous offensive about to be launched against them. When Joan was heard to cry, 'To the attack!', Dunois testified that those within the walls 'made their obedience to the Dauphin, shaking and trembling'.

After the usual negotiations had been carried out, the town surrendered peacefully and Charles was able to ride through the streets, with Joan at his side carrying her precious standard.

The last obstacle on the march to Reims was the town of Châlons-sur-Marne, towards which the army marched on Tuesday, 12 July. Here there was no resistance, and in response to the Dauphin's request to surrender peacefully, which was sent on ahead by a herald carrying Joan's standard, he was warmly welcomed by the bishop upon his arrival in the town on Thursday, 14 June, and—it was recorded—by the 'joyous inhabitants'.

It was at Châlons, towards which many people had travelled on their way to Reims for the coronation, that Joan met some of the villagers from Domremy, among them her godfather, Jean Moreau, to whom she made a present of the red dress she had worn when she left the village to journey to Vaucouleurs. She had imparted her secret thoughts about her departure from Domremy to Gérardin d'Epinal, stating, 'If you were not a Burgundian, I should tell you something'; she now told him, as he would later testify, that 'she feared nothing but treachery'—ominous words in the light of future events.

Leaving Châlons the following day, Wednesday, 13 July, the Dauphin and his court, with Joan at the head of the army, set off for the 30-mile march to Reims. Letters had been sent on ahead by the Archbishop of Reims and others, requesting the city to welcome Charles peacefully, and although Joan had assured him that no resistance would be offered, he was still somewhat apprehensive as to what kind of reception he would receive.

At a stop not far from Reims, at the castle of Sept-Saulx, officials from the city arrived to offer the Dauphin 'full and entire obedience', and the march then continued into Reims itself where, on Saturday, 16 July, the inhabitants came out to greet them with cries of 'Noel! Noel!', the traditional sign of acclaim associated with coronations from the time of Charlemagne.

The decision was taken for the coronation to take place at 9 o'clock on the following morning and, with less than 24 hours to prepare for the ceremony, a frenzy of activity followed. According to the records, everything possible was accomplished to enable the ceremonial procedure to be carried out with all the splendour attached to the sacring of the kings of France.

Early in the morning of Sunday, 17 July, four knights, known as the Guardians of the Holy Phial, rode to the Abbey of Saint-Rémy to receive the *sainte ampoule*, the holy oil, used since the time of Clovis for the consecration of French kings. They were greeted by the Abbé, who had managed to hide the precious object from the English, who had sacked the cathedral at the approach of the French, and had made off with much of the coronation regalia. (They would make use of this when, in 1431, Henry VI, the English boy king, was belatedly crowned King of France in Paris—a futile attempt since Charles was already acknowledged by all Frenchmen as the true king.)

The four knights returned to the cathedral, bearing the holy oil, and entered on horseback through the main door and past the great throng, where they were met by the Archbishop of Reims, and by canons, bishops and prelates who were preparing for the anointing of the new king.

The Dauphin entered the cathedral, accompanied by the Duke of Alençon, the Bastard of Orléans and Georges de la Trémoille, and with many other high-ranking members of his court and the army.

During the lengthy ceremony that followed, Joan stood beside the Dauphin, proudly holding her standard, and with her armour covered by a green tunic overlaid with a cloak of vermilion and gold—the livery of Orléans, ordered by the imprisoned Duke Charles in gratitude for her services to his city. At her trial, Joan was questioned about the role of her standard and why it had occupied such a significant position during the coronation ceremony. Her answer to the judges was that 'it had borne the burden, it was only right it should have the honour'.

At the end of the ceremony, when the crown had been placed on Charles' head and the 'Noels' and the trumpets had sounded forth 'as if to make the walls crumble', as one eyewitness said, Joan knelt before the King and, it was observed, amidst great emotion generated in those present, she embraced his legs, saying, 'Noble King, now is done God's pleasure, who willed me to raise the siege of Orléans and bring you to this city of Reims, showing that you are true King and him to whom the kingdom of God should belong.'

After the coronation was over, a great banquet was held in the Archbishop's palace, following which, Charles, wearing his crown, rode through the city to great acclaim from the crowds. He was accompanied by Joan, who was especially revered by the inhabitants, who flocked around her in great numbers, expressing their admiration and devotion.

7 Towards Paris

It was at Reims during the coronation ceremonies that Joan met her mother and father for the last time. They had travelled there, along with other villagers from Domremy, and one can only speculate on this reunion with their daughter. To see her in such elevated company, so fêted and, indeed, almost worshipped, must have seemed almost unbelievable to them, but in their few private moments together they undoubtedly found Joan to be the same simple and unchanged girl they had always known, in spite of the incredible events of the past months. Joan would certainly again express her contrition for leaving them so abruptly, and they would no doubt speak of the time when her mission would be over and she could return home.

That Joan herself thought of this as a distinct possibility at this point is testified to by Dunois in his evidence for the Rehabilitation, where he said that, after the coronation, during a triumphal ride at the King's side through one of the welcoming towns, he had overheard Joan express the wish, 'May it please God, my Maker, that I may now withdraw myself, leave off arms, and go and serve my father and my mother by keeping the sheep with my sister and my brothers who will rejoice so greatly to see me again.'

But if Joan's heartfelt wish had been fulfilled, their lives would have been vastly changed as, in December 1429, the King would ennoble Joan and her family, conferring upon them the title of *du Lys*, the documents making it clear that the succession would be transmitted to their descendants through both the male and female lines. Joan, of course, would never benefit from this honour, but her brothers would gain considerable status and many favours from Charles VII for the remainder of their lives. (It is now agreed that the du Lys line died out upon the death of Pierre's son, Jean, the sole descendant of the line.)

Bestowing noble rank upon Joan, which she had not requested, was an entirely spontaneous gesture by Charles, who for once was appreciative of her actions. It is indicative of Joan's nature that she never asked any favour for herself, but she did request Charles to grant exemption from taxes for the people of Domremy and its neighbour, Greux. The records, of which a copy still exists, state, *Néant, la Pucelle*, and the exemption was only brought to an end at the time of the French Revolution.

Following the success of her earlier victories, Joan was now more than ever determined that an attack on Paris should be undertaken without further delay. She was constantly troubled that her final task, to drive the English out of France, was far from being fulfilled, and she began to urge the King to begin the march to Paris, which was now under the joint control of the Duke of Bedford and his strong ally, the Duke of Burgundy.

Some time before the coronation, and in an effort at reconciliation, Charles had requested the presence of the Duke of Burgundy at the ceremony, but he had simply ignored the invitation. Joan had also sent him a letter, on the actual day of the ceremony, urging him, 'on behalf of the King of Heaven', to make peace between himself and Charles, in order to avoid spilling more French blood. Her letter was also ignored. What she did not know was that Charles, still very much under the influence of La Trémoille and the Archbishop of Reims, had entered into secret negotiations with Burgundy, who had agreed to a two-week truce, following which he had promised to surrender Paris to the King. How Charles could have believed in such an outlandish proposal is a total mystery, considering the failed negotiations and broken truces with Burgundy in the past.

The Duke of Bedford also made a pretence of honouring the truce, but both he and Burgundy were simply playing for time and were actually setting about a systematic fortification of the city. In fact, immediately after the battle of Patay, Bedford had called for reinforcements from England, and 3500 knights and archers had been shipped over to Calais early in July, then travelling on to Paris to arrive there towards the end of the month. Bedford also made the clever move of making Burgundy Governor of Paris, in the hope that he would be acceptable to the inhabitants—many of whom were unhappy with English rule—and would perhaps welcome the appointment of a prince of the French blood royal.

At Joan's continuing insistence that it was vital to begin the march towards Paris, the King finally appeared to respond, and he gave orders to make ready for the departure from Reims, which took place on Thursday, 21 July. However, it quickly became apparent that Charles was in no hurry to reach the capital, but was content to ride in triumph through the many towns that had capitulated to him without further resistance, following Joan's earlier successes in battle.

The first of many stops along the slow and convoluted route was made at Soissons, where the King 'was received with great joy by all', as indeed he was at Laon, Château-Thierry, Provins, Coulommiers and many other towns.

★ ★ ★

Whilst at Château-Thierry in July, when Joan was out riding through the countryside with the King, the crowds lining the route witnessed the extraordinary spectacle of clouds of butterflies encircling her standard. Possessed of immense spiritual energy, which emanated from an archangelic source, Joan always carried the great standard into battle to inspire the army to fight and achieve victory.

No mention has been made by biographers about the phenomenon of the butterflies, the episode no doubt being regarded as a curious but otherwise unimportant incident. But Rudolf Steiner's spiritual investigations into the inner relationship between the human and the animal kingdoms have revealed that butterflies are the oldest and most spiritual creatures in the insect world, and their delicate earthly forms are actually the miniature, physically metamorphosed forms of gigantic archangelic forms in the spiritual worlds—although not the archangelic beings themselves, but their metamorphosed images. In their earthly existence the butterflies live in the light-ether and it is their innate spiritual nature which caused them to be so irresistibly drawn into the radiant spiritual aura surrounding Joan's standard.

★ ★ ★

When the King eventually arrived at Crépy-en-Valois on Thursday, 11 August, he despatched his envoy to Compiègne, requesting the inhabitants to receive him 'obediently'; their subsequent reply indicated their willingness to do so.

Whilst at Crépy, Charles received a letter which was both challenging and defamatory to himself and to Joan. The letter was from the

Duke of Bedford, in which he stated that Charles was not the true king, as the young King Henry VI of England was the rightful heir to the French throne, and Charles wrongfully owed his position to 'a deranged and infamous woman, who dresses in men's clothes and is of a dissolute nature'. He ended his letter by summoning them both to meet him in battle at an early date near Senlis, to where the English army proceeded on 14 August.

The letter made Charles finally realize that he had been duped by the false promises of the surrender of Paris and, as Joan had maintained all along, the only course of action was to make an attack on the city as soon as possible.

As the French army headed towards Senlis, the English, although never far away, made no attempt to attack, arriving early in the day, on Sunday, 14 August, at Montepilloy, in an area not far from Senlis.

The French arrived there that same evening, and Joan immediately issued orders to make ready for battle on the following morning.

At dawn the next day, after hearing Mass, the French were eager to begin the fight and the army, some 6000–7000 strong, began the advance towards the English encampment. A number of minor skirmishes followed, but the main English army, though superior in numbers with between 8000–9000 men-at-arms, made no attempt to come out and fight, preferring to remain within their very strongly fortified defences.

Joan, anxious as always to do battle, rode out to the English positions with Alençon and the captains, openly striking the defences with her standard and challenging the English to come out and fight. When there was no reply, she called out that the French would even withdraw to allow the English time to prepare for battle. But there was still no response; the English felt safe behind their defences, and hoped the French would be the first to make the attack, but the French knew that an attempt on the English encampment, so strongly entrenched, would be disastrous. Each side knew the other's strengths, and the situation resulted in stalemate. If at this point Joan had been able to fight on the open battlefield, she was confident that victory would have been hers, in spite of the superior strength of the enemy. She would then have been able to march on Paris, sure in the knowledge that it would fall to her. As it turned out, the events at Montepilloy were a hollow victory, contributing in no small measure to her defeat before Paris, a defeat which would be a major factor in her declining fortunes.

The Duke of Bedford had, in fact, decided to move the army back to Paris, and the French awoke next morning to find the battlefield totally deserted. Joan would certainly have wished to make pursuit and engage them in battle but, much against her wishes, Charles decided to withdraw the army to Compiègne.

When they arrived in Compiègne on Thursday, 18 August, it was to an enthusiastic welcome by the major dignitaries, headed by the Captain of the town, Guillaume de Flavy. The reception accorded to Charles was such that he was happy to stay and enjoy the lavish hospitality, and he remained in Compiègne until the end of that month.

Joan was desperately unhappy during the time at Compiègne, and constantly urged the King to move on Paris. Her entreaties became even more persistent when news reached them that the Duke of Bedford had been obliged to leave the city with a considerable force, in order to quell a rebellion in the Rouen area. This news prompted Joan to tell Alençon, 'Make yourself ready, for by my *martin*, I want to go to see Paris from closer than I have ever seen it.'

At this point, Georges de la Trémoille was advising Charles against making the attack on Paris, but at Joan's continuing insistence the King eventually relented and, on Monday, 23 August, she was finally able to set out for the city with the army, accompanied as always by Alençon and all the captains who had fought with her in the Loire campaign. The size of the army is not known, but it was considerably enlarged along the route by troops who had been stationed at Senlis, following the surrender of the city to the French.

The march to Paris took three days, and upon her arrival on the outskirts Joan camped on the heights of Saint-Denis, from where she could see the city and its fortifications. Reputed to be the most strongly fortified in the whole of Europe, its massive walls were over eight metres high, entirely encircling the city and surrounded by a deep, wide moat.

The task facing Joan was enormous; unlike the towns she had captured in the Loire, which were relatively small in size, a large city like Paris could not be encircled, even by the largest army. But Joan, as always, believed that God would aid her. Almost immediately upon her arrival she sent out reconnoitring parties, whilst at the same time constantly bombarding sections of the city walls with her heavy artillery, in order to test the defences. Alençon meanwhile ordered a bridge to be built at one point over the moat.

All the time these preparatory actions were taking place, Joan was anticipating the King's arrival, as without his permission the main attack could not begin. But Charles failed to arrive and Alençon had twice to ride to Senlis, where the King had moved from Compiègne. At Alençon's first visit Charles had promised he would leave for Paris, but failed to keep his word, and it was only at the Duke's second attempt that he reluctantly agreed to accompany him to Saint-Denis.

Upon his arrival there, on Wednesday, 7 September, plans were quickly made by the captains for an attack on the city on the following day, the decision being taken that, of the six gates situated at points along the walls, the assault would be centred on the Saint-Honoré gate.

Joan spent the night in vigil in the parish church of the village of La Chapelle, where the army was encamped, and after Mass and Holy Communion the next morning, she led the army towards the city. Several strategies had been put in place by Alençon, following which the attack commenced around midday, with a first bombardment of the walls. Carrying her standard, Joan led the attack and moved close to the walls.

Although the assault was intense, very little headway was made and the army suffered heavy counter-attacks from the defenders, from cannon and other heavy missiles. With fierce assaults on both sides continuing throughout the day, Joan's soldiers had made barely any impact on the walls, enduring an ever more intensive bombardment from within.

Towards sunset, Joan, accompanied by her standard bearer, advanced towards the moat in order to test the depth of the water with a lance, hoping to make a further, final assault of the day from a slightly different point of attack. It was then that she was hit in the thigh by a bolt from a crossbow. Her standard bearer was also wounded, and as he raised his visor in order to remove the arrow, he was fatally shot between the eyes.

Some of the captains rushed to Joan's aid, and despite her repeated protestations that another attack would have been successful, they decided to carry her back to the camp, insisting that the hour was late and the army tired.

On the following morning, and despite her serious wound, Joan insisted that another attack should be made, and she urged Alençon to make the army ready, declaring that she would never leave Paris until the city had been taken. But as preparations were under way, envoys came from the King with orders that Joan should meet up with him at Saint-Denis.

Annoyed and angry at this delay, Joan rode to meet the King, only to learn that he had ordered the destruction of the bridge built by Alençon, thereby making their planned attack at a specific point along the city walls impossible. The reason for this, Charles informed Joan, was that, in any case he had decided to halt any further action.

Joan was totally devastated by Charles' decision and also unable to understand the reason for this unexpected action, but what she and the captains did not know was that, in August, Charles had made a further, four-month-long treaty with the Anglo-Burgundian party, which had been negotiated by La Trémoille, and by others who had the King's ear.

It is obvious that Charles had sent Joan and the army to certain defeat. As the euphoria he had experienced following his coronation passed, his gratitude to Joan disappeared also. His base nature began to reassert itself, and he was notorious for his changeable attitude to those in his service; as one contemporary chronicle observed: 'with those he had raised high, he could, by a whim, wilfully reverse that person from high to low'.

For Joan, there was nothing to be done but to obey the King's command to withdraw, and her final act, as she told the judges at her trial, was in the abbey of Saint-Denis, where she offered up a suit of white armour taken from a captured Burgundian knight, 'as was the custom among men-of-war after being wounded, and because Saint-Denis is the war cry of France'.

8 Victory—and Defeat

There was little a frustrated Joan could do at this point, other than obey the King's command and follow him and the army in the retreat from Paris. Charles had decided to travel to Gien in the Loire and it was there, later in September, that he gave the order to disband the army. This was obviously a great blow for Joan, who could see her third objective, 'to drive the English out of France', becoming ever more remote.

Her frustration and disappointment were further compounded when the King dismissed Joan's greatest friend and ally, her *beau duc*, Alençon, ordering him back to his estates and his family. When Joan had promised his wife that she would send him back safely to her, she could never have imagined that it would be under such circumstances.

This act by Charles was another devastating blow to Joan's mission, and a further step towards her now declining fortunes. Some months later Alençon attempted a reunion with Joan and petitioned the King to allow her to join him in Normandy, where he was engaged in fighting an English force, but Charles refused and they were never to meet again.

During the period that followed, Joan was ordered to live under the supervision of Charles d'Albret, the King's governor in Berry. It is not without significance that d'Albret was the half-brother of La Trémoille who, as ever, jealous of Joan's influence with the King, was undoubtedly responsible for her move away from the court into a situation where he could be informed of her activities at all times.

Accompanied by d'Albret and his retinue, Joan moved through various towns to great acclaim. First she went to Bourges, where she stayed for three weeks in the house of the King's financial adviser, René de Bouligny. His wife, Marguerite La Touroulde, became Joan's close friend, sharing a bed with her, as was the custom, and visiting the baths together. She would testify to the Rehabilitation tribunal to Joan's purity and simplicity of nature. She also stated that Joan was frequently asked by devout townspeople to bless their rosaries and other religious objects, but said that Joan would laugh at such requests and simply say, 'Touch them yourselves, your touch will do as much good as mine.'

Later, at Montfauçon-en-Berry, she was visited by a so-called prophetess, Catherine de La Rochelle, who had been sent to her by Brother Richard, the dubious friar whom Joan had met at Troyes. Catherine claimed that, like Joan, she had visions and revelations, and told Joan that she was able to influence the King and return Joan to armed combat. But Joan was suspicious and consulted her two saints, Catherine and Margaret, who told her that the woman was an impostor, whereupon Joan advised her to go home to her husband. Catherine would later be denounced by the Inquisition in Paris.

During this period of relative inactivity, Joan may have learned to read and write a little, but as she stated at her trial, 'I know not A from B.' She did, however, learn to sign her name. Her signature, a large, scrawling 'Jehanne', can still be seen today in surviving letters dictated by her in 1429 and 1430 to the dignitaries of various 'good towns' asking for their support for the King in retaking territories still in the hands of the enemy.

By October, 1429, the King had settled with his court at the château of Mehun-sur-Yèvre, near Bourges, where Joan again urged him to send her to fight the enemy in the north. Much to her great dismay, however, she was informed that she would only be allowed to accompany a small army to attack Saint-Pierre-le-Moutier, a town some 50 miles to the south, which was under the control of a notorious and powerful mercenary, Perrinet Bressart.

Bressart had long been employed by the English and the Burgundians to hold the region for them, but he had eventually gained such dominance there that he had even become a serious threat to his masters.

Behind these plans to send Joan to attack Bressart was the ever wily La Trémoille who, in 1427, had been on a mission to negotiate with Bressart about his constant raiding of the province of Berry. But instead of meeting the mercenary under the terms of an agreed safe conduct, Bressart had captured and imprisoned him and demanded a huge ransom for his freedom. La Trémoille had obviously never forgotten this humiliating episode and would certainly have advised the King who tired of Joan's entreaties was no doubt happy to be rid of her. In sending Joan against Bressart, La Trémoille was aware that either she or Bressart might be captured or even killed; in either case, his hatred of Bressart and his ever-growing antagonism towards Joan would give him some form of vengeance.

The army was marshalled at Bourges and set off to attempt to regain, firstly, Saint-Pierre-le-Moutier, and then head to La Charité-sur-Loire, where Bressart had his headquarters.

The town of Saint-Pierre-le-Moutier, although small, was heavily fortified; entirely surrounded by strong walls and a deep moat, and with the extra protection of six towers and strengthened gates, it was by no means an easy target.

The army, headed by Charles d'Albret, arrived towards the end of October, and was positioned around the town. Initial attacks by the French made little headway, because of the fierce resistance by the large numbers of defenders. The French efforts were further undermined by the lack of heavy weaponry, bombards and the like, which Joan had always used to great effect in sieges of a similar nature.

The first days of November were without success, but Joan took the decision to storm the fortifications once more. Again, the assault was unsuccessful and the army was forced to retreat.

It is to Joan's faithful squire, Jean d'Aulon, that we owe the account of the events that followed. In his deposition for the Rehabilitation he gave the following testimony:

> At this time, having been severely wounded in the heel by an arrow, so that I was unable to stand or walk, I saw that the Maid had been left with a small company of her men and I felt that harm would ensue. I quickly mounted a horse and rushed towards her. I asked her what she was doing there alone like that, and why she had not retired with the rest. After removing her helmet, she said that she was not alone and that she still had in her company fifty thousand of her men and would not leave the spot until she had taken the town. At that time, whatever she might say, she had not more than five men with her and I entreated her once more that she should retreat, but she cried out loudly, 'Bring faggots and hurdles, everyone, to build a bridge,' which was immediately done. At this I marvelled

greatly, for immediately the town was taken by storm, and there was no great resistance.

More than 25 years later, d'Aulon could still marvel at the events he had witnessed at Joan's side, and to his lengthy testimony he added: 'All the Maid's exploits seemed to me divine and miraculous, and it would have been impossible for anyone as young as the Maid to perform such deeds except at the will and guidance of Our Lord.'

Joan's mystifying account to d'Aulon, that she had thousands of her soldiers fighting with her, has sometimes been interpreted to mean that her vision was of legions of protecting angels. However, Rudolf Steiner has pointed out that, to those with spiritual sight, it can be observed that when men die in battle the forces of the etheric body are still unexpended, and they continue to fight on.

The victory at Saint-Pierre-le-Moutier was to be Joan's last triumph. The next task facing her, to lay siege to La Charité-sur-Loire, presented enormous difficulties, as the essential army equipment which had in any case been inadequate for Saint-Pierre was now even more depleted. Requests by Joan and d'Albret to the King for reinforcements met with no response and the only course open to them was to send letters to various loyal towns, requesting their help in supplying gunpowder, arms and money.

Joan's letter, written from her headquarters at Moulins on 9 November to the citizens of Riom, shows the desperation she felt at their situation. Part of her letter read, 'I beseech you that you love and honour your King . . . that you immediately send help for this siege . . .' Joan's letter, possibly the first to bear her signature, a rather poorly executed scrawl, is still kept in the town's archives to this day. The Johannic scholar Jules Quicherat saw the letter with its red seal, into which was embedded a fingerprint, and a single black hair, a custom of the day representing the sender's personal mark. Unfortunately, the hair has since disappeared, appropriated, it is thought, by an unscrupulous souvenir hunter.

Some of the towns did respond; Riom offered a gift of money—but failed to send it on when asked, although other towns did manage to send some arms and the much needed gunpowder. Further away, the city of Orléans, hearing of Joan's plight, and ever grateful to her for saving the city, sent men-at-arms and artillery held from the earlier campaigns. Although these efforts were not enough to satisfactorily reinforce the army, the somewhat reluctant decision was nevertheless taken to begin the attack on La Charité on 14 November.

At the start of the offensive even the weather was against the French, as winter had arrived early and it was bitterly cold. The town was very heavily fortified and access to the walls could only be gained by a single bridge across the Loire.

During the month that followed, and despite daily attacks, the French failed in their attempts to breach the walls. Eventually, the cold and exhausted army was withdrawn and the long march back to the north began. Laying the blame with the King for failing to assist the army, a chronicler reporting the events wrote that 'they withdrew with great displeasure'.

Nothing is known of Joan's activities during the siege of La Charité. At her trial, she would deny having been sent there by her Heavenly Counsel. When asked by her accusers, 'Why did you not enter into the town, since you had God's commandment to do so?,' Joan replied, 'Who told you that I had God's commandment?' And to their question, 'Did your Voices give you counsel?', she answered, 'I wanted to go into France, but the captains said it was better to go first to La Charité.'

9 Capture

After the failure at La Charité, Joan had no other choice but to rejoin the King at Mehun-sur-Yèvre. At Christmas she was in Jargeau, where she received the documents informing her of her ennoblement, the official wording of which thanked her for her 'praiseworthy, graceful and useful services already rendered ... which we hope to pursue in future'. But, despite the praise contained in these words, it is doubtful if Charles was sincere about any future deeds he would allow Joan to perform for his kingdom. He remained totally apathetic to her constant pleas to carry out the last part of her mission, 'to drive the English out of France', and in conferring the great honour of her ennoblement he may have hoped that she would be content to rest on her laurels, or possibly even decide to return to her home.

In January, 1430, Joan was at the château of Sully-sur-Loire, the home of La Trémoille, who was continually plotting to keep her as far away from the King as possible, and had undoubtedly arranged for her to be sent there.

A brief respite from her incarceration at Sully came later in the month, when she was invited to attend a banquet in Orléans, together with one of her brothers, possibly Pierre, as he was frequently at her side during her campaigns. While in Orléans she met with friends and acquaintances she had known at Poitiers and Tours in the previous year. Amongst these was a man for whom she had a special regard, the Scotsman, Hamish Power, to whom she had entrusted the making and design of her beloved standard. Power had a daughter about to be married, and Joan arranged for a gift of money to be paid to him towards the cost of the wedding.

During the following months, Joan had to content herself by sending supportive letters to some of the northern towns in danger of attack from English and Burgundian forces. Two of her letters were sent to Reims in March, which was facing a threatened siege by the Burgundians. Some of the inhabitants were in favour of surrender without a fight, but in both her letters Joan sought to reassure them that if they should be attacked she would go to their aid, adding in one letter that she would make their enemies 'put on their spurs so fast that they will not know how [be able] to put them on [fast enough] and get out of there and very quickly at that'.

These were brave words and certainly full of sincerity on Joan's part, but it is extremely doubtful that she would have been able to carry them out. Aside from Charles' continuing apathy to fight, the enemy forces were too strong in the northern territories and were, in fact, becoming ever more powerful. Charles was again attempting to arrange what would eventually turn out to be yet another ill-fated treaty with the Duke of Burgundy who, at this point, was refusing to arrange for its commencement.

The Duke of Bedford was meanwhile amassing a huge army, by bringing 2000 fighting men over from England, an action which would be followed in April when the boy king, Henry VI, arrived in Calais. He had been crowned King of England in November of the previous year, and the intention was to crown him King of France in Paris, in defiance of the crowning of Charles VII in Reims.

In February, the King left Mehun for Sully, where Joan joined him in March. She must have been even more determined to go and do battle, when she heard that there were a number of successful uprisings against the English and Burgundians by the inhabitants of cities and towns in the north. She was particularly concerned about the town of Compiègne, which the King had actually ordered to surrender to the Duke of Burgundy in the previous September, as part of an agreement made with him to hand over certain towns under an earlier treaty. Compiègne, however, refused to surrender and the Governor, Guillaume de Flavy, had begun to strengthen the fortifications and rearm the town in readiness for the impending siege.

It is believed that Joan left Sully, either at the end of March or the beginning of April, on what would be her last mission. Records differ as to whether she had the King's permission or left without his knowledge. It is known that she was accompanied by her squire, d'Aulon, and her brother, Pierre, but she no longer had the splendid military household she had previously possessed, and the company she headed was very small. The troops were under the direction of a mercenary, Barthélemy Baretta, with some 200 Italians, possibly also mercenaries.

The small army set off for Lagny-sur-Marne, via Melun, which was on the road to Compiègne. It was while at Melun at Easter, on 22 April, that Joan learned from her saints of her impending capture. At her trial she told the judges '... it was told me by the voices of St Catherine and St Margaret that I should be taken by St John's Day and that so it must be and that I be not dismayed, and take all in good part and that God would help me.' She added that, from this point, she told no one about the revelation she had received and submitted herself 'above all in the matter of war to the will of the captains'.

At Lagny Joan encountered a band of Anglo-Burgundian fighters, led by a notorious mercenary, Franquet d'Arras. Confident that he was able to defeat the famous Maid, d'Arras engaged in a fierce battle with Joan's forces, but was quickly defeated, due to her superiority in numbers and clever strategy. D'Arras was taken hostage and it was Joan's intention to have him exchanged for a French prisoner, but when she was informed that the latter had already been executed by the enemy, she handed d'Arras over to the Bailiff in Senlis, who tried and subsequently executed him on a charge of treason. This episode was to lead to accusations at Joan's trial that she had caused d'Arras to be murdered, but she defiantly insisted that she was justified in giving him up to the authorities at Senlis, because of the execution of the Frenchman.

Another incident occurred at Lagny, which was also brought up against Joan at her trial. This concerned her involvement in the apparent restoring to life of a three-day-old baby who had shown no signs of life since its birth. Joan stated that she had prayed with the women of the town before the local statue of the Virgin Mary for the child to be given life. The child appeared to revive and yawned three times, whereupon it was immediately baptized, and although it then died, it was allowed to be buried in holy ground. Joan's accusers were trying to prove that she had used sorcery to bring the child back to life, but she was insistent that she had simply prayed along with the others.

Departing from Lagny, Joan and the army reached Senlis on 24 April, to learn that the Duke of Burgundy was successfully attacking various towns on his way to lay siege to Compiégne, the most important town in the region, which was known as 'the gateway into

France'. Her words at this time were, 'I must go and see my good friends at Compiégne.'

Joan entered Compiégne on 13 May and made her way to the church of Saint-Jacques, where she heard Mass and took Communion, as was her usual custom. It was in the church that she told the large numbers of townspeople who had gathered to see her, 'My good friends, I am sold and betrayed. Soon I shall be given up to death. Pray to God for me, for I can no longer serve the King and the kingdom of France.' On the following day she was honoured with a reception and banquet by the town's dignitaries.

On 16 May, Burgundy began his siege of Compiégne, having dispersed his enormous army at key positions in the vicinity of the town. Extant accounts record that he had large numbers of every kind of weaponry, including siege engines, bombards and cannon. Even so, the town was a magnificent example of medieval fortification. Its walls were thick and high and entirely surrounded the town. A large number of towers were situated at key points along the walls, many of which ran parallel to the river Oise, which served as a moat on one side of the town, while its waters filled a deep and wide ditch which had been excavated and the soil used as a rampart to add to the defences. A large number of gates, protected by gatehouses, led into the town, and the single bridge over the river was also fortified with strong defences along its length.

Compiégne itself was also heavily armed and therefore able to withstand prolonged attack. The siege of the town would, in fact, continue until the following October, when Burgundy was forced to withdraw, following a successful attack by French forces.

Joan made daily sorties out of Compiégne to meet the enemy, most notably to the village of Choisy-le-Bac to the north-west. A bridge crossed the Aisne river at this spot, which was being held by Louis, the brother of the Governor, Guillaume Flavy, and the hope was that if the French could hold this important site it would prevent the Burgundians from encircling Compiégne entirely. But the Burgundian forces, with much heavier artillery, fought ferociously. After heavy casualties on both sides, the French were forced to withdraw.

A further sortie was made on 18 May in the area of Soissons, with the intention of attacking the Burgundians from the rear. Although

Soissons was a French-held town, the Governor, Guichard Bournel, soon made it clear that he and the inhabitants were not prepared to fight in its defence. Entry to Joan's forces was refused, but Joan and her captains were allowed into the town, while the army remained encamped outside in the fields. The next day the French were reluctantly obliged to return to Compiégne.

Two days later, Joan rode south to Crépy-en-Valois to meet up with some 500 soldiers who had volunteered to fight in the defence of Compiégne. Upon returning on the night of 22 May, they found that the town was entirely surrounded by the English and Burgundian armies. Some of the men were hesitant about attempting to pass through the enemy lines with their relatively small force, but Joan convinced them, saying, 'By my *martin*, we are sufficient, and I must go to my good friends in Compiégne.' Because of the many gates into the town, they were able to gain entry in the early hours of 23 May.

Eager as always to fight, Joan was now convinced that there was no time to be lost in attacking the enemy and, without resting, she began preparations for a foray outside the town, with a large mounted force. As they rode towards the fields outside Compiégne at 9 o'clock in the morning, on what was to be her last day of freedom, there is a wonderfully descriptive word-picture of Joan's appearance and bearing, recorded by the Burgundian chronicler Georges Chastellain who, though not present at the time, would soon be well informed of the day's events by her captors:

> She mounted her horse, armed as would a man, and adorned with a doublet of rich cloth-of-gold over her armour. She rode a dapple-grey charger, very handsome and very proud, and displayed herself in her armour and in her conduct as would a captain who led a large army. And thus arrayed, and with her standard raised high and blowing in the wind, and accompanied by many noble men, she sallied forth from the town.

Joan's first attack, on the village of Margny, to the south-west of Compiégne, was successful and the Burgundians fled in disorder. As they retreated they were joined by the forces of Jean de Luxembourg, a powerful ally of Burgundy, who was stationed at Clairoix to the east of the town, where he had heard of their retreat, and came to assist with his large army. With the English army positioned at Venette, south-west of the town, and the Burgundian army to the north, their huge forces were thus combined to begin the attack on the French. Joan said at her trial that she had clashed with the enemy three times, only to be finally overwhelmed by the relentless onslaught directed against them. The French were forced to retreat along the river bank towards the town.

The final enemy charge succeeded in isolating Joan and a small company from the main body of the army, but she continued to engage Luxembourg's forces in an attempt to protect her army's retreat. Chastellain recorded, 'The Maid, going beyond the nature of womankind, performed a great feat and took much pain to save her company from loss.'

The main body of the French army, hotly pursued by the enemy, were just able to reach the town, but once they were safely inside, Guillaume de Flavy, seeing the great numbers of the enemy about to cross the river, ordered the drawbridge to be raised and the gates shut. Joan and her small band were left outside to face the enemy alone.

The act of closing off Joan's only escape route by de Flavy has been the subject of much debate by Johannic writers during the last two centuries. Even in the fifteenth century, accounts by various chroniclers were undecided as to whether de Flavy had been bribed to purposely close the gates to prevent Joan from escaping her enemies or if his action was solely to prevent the enemy from entering the town. Joan had previously said that she 'feared nothing but treason', and those who have held the former view have quoted the fact that de Flavy had been appointed as Governor of Compiègne by Joan's enemy, La Trémoille, who would certainly have been pleased to have her caught. De Flavy was also a relation of another of Joan's opponents, Regnault de Chartres. The Archbishop had, in fact, been present in Compiègne a few days before Joan was captured. Those who support the view that de Flavy had simply acted to protect the town from invasion cite his loyalty to the King in his long career as a soldier and his excellent record as a dedicated Governor of Compiègne.

Joan was now in a totally hopeless situation. Pursued relentlessly by the huge forces of the enemy, who were determined to take her at all costs, her capture was inevitable. As she headed in the direction of the town, fighting desperately all the way, a party of Luxembourg's men closed in upon her. Although continuing to offer resistance, she was finally surrounded by a small group who, despite the efforts of her immediate companions to fight them off, were able to bring her horse to a standstill. Then, as Chastellain recorded, 'An archer, a rough and very sour man, full of much spite that a woman about whom much had been spoken should have defeated so many valiant men, seized the edge of her cloth-of-gold doublet and dragged her from her horse flat upon the ground.'

This archer was in the service of Lionel, the Bastard of Wandomme, an officer under Jean de Luxembourg, who arrived on the scene and, under the laws of chivalry, accepted Joan's surrender and her oath that she would not attempt to escape.

The Bastard, 'happier than if he had captured a king', took Joan and other prisoners, including her brother, Pierre, and her squire, Jean d'Aulon, to Luxembourg's camp at Margny. Upon being informed of Joan's capture, the Duke of Burgundy hastened there, anxious to see the prized captive for himself. Some words were exchanged between them, although there is no record of the actual conversation that took place. But it was recorded that great rejoicing continued into the night among the Burgundians and English who, celebrating the day's events, 'were more joyful than if they had taken five hundred of the enemy'.

Joan knew that she would eventually be captured, as she had been told by her Voices at Melun in April. At her trial she stated that they had repeatedly said this would happen and she had implored them to tell her when, and that she might die quickly rather than languish in prison, but they had not told her when she would be captured. Further questioned that if her Heavenly Counsel had told her to go out of Compiègne on that fateful day and that she would be taken, she replied that she would not have gone willingly, but would have obeyed their command whatever the outcome.

It is clear that Joan's Spiritual Counsel had not instructed her to fight on that day. Perhaps they wished to spare her the anguish of knowing in advance of the impending ordeal of her capture. Nevertheless, she did go out and confront the enemy and, although she was defeated on that day, her capture caused her enemies to break off their attack on

Compiègne, a place of such strategic importance for the defence of the region that, had it fallen to the opposing forces, it could have caused serious hindrance to the long-term plan by the Divine Powers working for the future of European civilization. A vital part of this plan was to expel the English nation with its crusading but misdirected impulse from the soil of France and cause it to return to its island, from where it could then pursue its rightful and predestined path.

After the great victory at Orléans, Christine de Pisan, in a line from her inspired poem about Joan and the plight of France, has Joan challenge the enemy with the words, 'Do you want to fight against God?' But those powers working against the true forces of evolution had prevailed, and the earthly mission of the one who played such a vital role at the beginning of the new impulse for Europe was brought to an end.

10   The Final Journey

News of Joan's capture on 23 May 1430 was quickly spread throughout France. On the same day, the Duke of Burgundy wrote the first of a number of letters addressed to various Anglo-Burgundian sympathizers, recounting the event. The triumphant tone of one such letter began: 'By the pleasure of our blessed Creator, the woman called the Maid has been taken; and from her capture will be recognized the error and mad belief of all those who became sympathetic and favourable to the deeds of this woman...'

The news reached Paris on 25 May where it was recorded in the register of Parliament by the Clerk, Clément de Fauquembergue. From the time of the fall of the city in 1418, the clergy of the University of Paris, powerful in both political and theological life, had been totally committed to the Anglo-Burgundian cause, and had kept Joan in their sights from the time she came into prominence; in May 1429, following the victory at Orléans, they had expressed their opinion that Joan's victories were due to heresy. They lost no time in writing to the Duke of Burgundy, on 26 May, in the name of the Inquisitor of France, Jean Graverent, demanding that Joan be handed over to them with out delay: '...that the soonest and most safely and conveniently it can be done, be sent and brought prisoner to us the said Joan, since she is strongly suspected of many crimes smacking of heresy...' But Burgundy was in no hurry to give Joan up as he had other, more lucrative plans for her surrender. Although the University would make more demands in the following months, Joan was not to be delivered up to the city which had been the scene of her first defeat; instead, she would face a long and circuitous journey, which would finally lead to Rouen, and to the place of her trial and martyrdom.

Joan's bitter enemy at court, Regnault de Chartres, wrote to the citizens of his diocese at Reims, in a spiteful vein, informing them that her capture had been brought about by her refusal to accept counsel, her pride in wearing rich garments, and by not doing God's will, but her own.

But there were many areas in France sympathetic to Joan's plight, where the clergy asked for special prayers to be said for her deliverance. The Archbishop of Embrun, Jacques Gelu, even wrote to the King: 'For the recovery of this girl, and for her ransom, let neither money nor possessions be spared, whatever be the price asked, so that Your Majesty may not incur the undying shame of basest ingratitude. Get people everywhere to pray, and you yourself pray also, so that if this misfortune has come upon us because of any sin of the King, or people of France, it may please God to forgive it.' What, if any, was Charles' response to the Archbishop's bold request is unknown, but prayers alone would not be enough to free Joan. Charles could possibly have sent an armed force to rescue her from her captors, but there were difficulties in attempting any attack on the strongly held Anglo-Burgundian territories. However, it would soon become clear that he had no intention of sending aid to Joan; his treacherous behaviour to those he had previously favoured was well known. It was enough for him that Joan had made him King—she was now of no further use to him.

In Joan's short career her fame had not only spread throughout France, as there is also testimony to the great interest in her exploits across the whole of Europe. In the following year, as far away as Constantinople, the Emperor and his court were reported as being 'greatly astonished to learn of her capture and fate'.

Joan and her captors now began what was to be a seven-month-long journey, its duration and route being necessary in order to bypass certain towns whose inhabitants, although subject to Anglo-Burgundian rule, were far from happy with their situation, and where there was the possibility of disruptive elements and even uprising, which might result in escape by the prisoner. There was also the threat of encounters with the many roaming bands of Armagnac resistance along the route.

From Luxembourg's camp at Margny, Joan was taken by way of Clairoix and Beauvoir to Luxembourg's château of Beaulieu-les-Fontaines near Noyon, at the end of May. Here she was visited by the Duke of Burgundy and his wife, Isabelle of Portugal, who had expressed a desire to see her. This was the first of many visits during Joan's long journey, when the interested or merely curious were drawn to see the famous Maid.

It was at Beaulieu that Joan made her first attempt to escape. She was imprisoned on the first floor of the château, and her squire, d'Aulon, was allowed to visit her. Guards were placed outside her room, but she was not chained or bound. During a night in early June, she must have been pacing around the room when she noticed some loose floorboards. She then managed to lift enough of the boarding to let herself down to the ground floor, where she found herself at the main entrance of the château, beside which was a room used by the sentries on duty. Seeing the keys on the outside of the door, she was about to lock the sentries in, when she was surprised by the night porter, who raised the alarm. She was then thrown into a small, dark cell to await the next stage of her journey. Questioned at her trial about her escape attempt, she replied that she would always attempt to escape, but 'that it did not please God that I should escape that time'.

At the end of June or beginning of July, Joan was transferred some 40 miles further north to Jean de Luxembourg's main home, the château-fortress of Beaurevoir, situated in what was then extensive woodland between Cambrai and Saint-Quentin, where she would remain until November. Here, her situation was made less onerous by the presence of three more Joans: Luxembourg's wife, Jeanne de Béthune, her daughter from a previous marriage, Jeanne de Bar, and Luxembourg's aunt, the aged Jeanne de Luxembourg, who was the matriarch of this powerful family.

These three ladies showed great kindness to Joan, but they were no doubt rather shocked by her male dress and offered to give her women's clothing. But Joan refused, and when questioned about this at her trial she replied, 'I would have done so willingly at the request of these ladies, but I had not permission from God.' Her insistence to retain her male attire was no doubt reinforced by the attitude of some of the men with whom she was forced to associate. One man, who gave evidence at the Trial of Rehabilitation, was Haimond de Macy, at the time a knight in the service of Jean de Luxembourg. He testified that he often saw Joan at Beaurevoir and frequently conversed with her, and, 'I tried several times, playfully to touch her breasts, which Joan would not allow, and she repulsed me with all her strength.'

It was at Beaurevoir that Joan made her second attempt at freedom, when she leapt from a high tower of the château. Closely questioned at her trial about this, she gave two reasons for her attempted escape: 'I had heard that all in Compiègne down to the age of seven years were to be put to fire and to the sword, and I preferred to die rather than live after such destruction of good people... And the other was that I knew I was sold to the English and I would rather have died than to be in the hands of the English, my enemies.' Asked if she had made the leap on the advice of her Voices: 'Catherine told me almost every day that I must not leap and that God would help me and also them of Compiègne,' and, 'Without fail, you must accept your lot.' 'But when I heard that the English were coming to take me ... I leapt and commended myself to God and the Virgin Mary, and I was injured in that leap. And after I had leapt, the voice of St Catherine told me to be of good countenance and that the people of Compiègne would receive succour.'

This extraordinary, but desperate attempt to escape from what was, apparently, an 18-metre-high tower left Joan severely concussed, and she was found concussed on the ground. She would tell her judges that she could neither eat nor drink for two or three days, but was comforted by St Catherine who told her to confess and ask God's forgiveness, and that the people of Compiègne would have succour before St Martin's Day (11 November). This prediction was fulfilled when Jean de Luxembourg and his army made a fierce attack on the town on 24 October, but suffered a decisive defeat by the French and had to withdraw in great disarray, leaving behind most of their heavy artillery. Joan must certainly have been happy and relieved to hear of this victory for her 'good friends of Compiègne', in whose cause she had so valiantly fought on the fateful day of her capture.

Immediately after her capture, a powerful individual began the relentless pursuit of a course intended to secure Joan's release into the hands of the University of Paris and its English masters. This man was Pierre Cauchon, Bishop of Beauvais, who would prove to be Joan's most implacable enemy. From his youth, Cauchon had sought by every means in his power to rise ever higher in the religious and political life of the time. A former Rector of the University, he had played a leading role in convincing its members to take the side of the Burgundians against the Armagnacs. He had also been involved in promoting the theory of a double monarchy, whereby both France and England would be ruled by England alone. Following his successful negotiations during the Treaty of Troyes, he was made Bishop of Beauvais in 1420. He was living in Reims up to the time of Charles VII's coronation, but had to make a hurried exit from the city and later was forced to flee from Beauvais when the town went over to the French. He had high hopes of being appointed to the vacant archbishopric of Rouen, as a reward for his services—an office to which he was never raised, remaining Bishop of Beauvais for the rest of his life.

Spurred on by the increasing demands of the University, and by a desire to avenge his humiliation of twice being driven from his home as a result of Joan's successes, Cauchon now travelled extensively in his attempts to procure her release into English hands. Starting his four-month journey from Paris in June, he went first to Calais where the Duke of Bedford was staying with the young King Henry VI. In Calais, arrangements were made to fix Joan's ransom at 6000 *livres* (pounds), with the proviso that it could be raised as high as 10,000, the sum which would, in fact, ultimately be paid for her.

From Calais, Cauchon met up with Jean de Luxembourg and the Duke of Burgundy at Luxembourg's camp near Compiègne at the beginning of July, where he made an unsuccessful attempt to negotiate Joan's ransom. It was here that he had a meeting with Jeanne de Luxembourg, following which they both travelled on to Beaurevoir, where a conversation took place with Joan present. Details of this meeting and Joan's participation in the discussion are unknown, but the elderly Jeanne had always shown the greatest sympathy towards Joan, and it appears that it was she who firmly held out against handing her over at this point. As the head of the family, Jeanne also held the keys to the family fortune and had earlier that year informed her nephew that she intended drawing up her will and, although undecided in favour of other family members, she had hinted that he might be the sole beneficiary. It was therefore vital that he should not risk the displeasure of this powerful lady. Also, Luxembourg knew full well the value of his prisoner and may have hoped that delaying tactics could bring a higher price for Joan later on.

At the end of July, Cauchon was in Rouen, where he again met up with Bedford and the young King, and further negotiations were carried out to increase the amount of Joan's ransom. At the end of

September, the sum of 765 *livres* was paid to Cauchon by the Receiver General of Normandy, Pierre Surreau, for 'seven score and thirteen days ... spent in the service of the King'. By 24 October, coincidentally the day of the liberation of Compiègne, the remaining ransom money had been raised by the English treasurer, Thomas Blount.

Meanwhile, having decided in favour of her nephew, Jeanne de Luxembourg made her will, in which she left him her entire estate. She died shortly afterwards, leaving a much relieved Luxembourg free to go ahead with his plans to sell his prisoner.

From Beaurevoir, Joan was taken further north, to Arras, where she was imprisoned in the Cour le Comte, the stronghold of the Dukes of Burgundy, and where she would remain until Luxembourg could negotiate the terms of her release into English hands. Whilst at Arras she was visited by Jean de Pressy, Chamberlain to the Duke of Burgundy, who tried to persuade her to wear women's dress but, as she had refused the request by the ladies of the Luxembourg household, she again refused to change from her male attire.

Although Joan may have felt relatively safe at Beaurevoir, after leaving there her conditions of imprisonment became more severe, as she would never again be allowed to have women with her. Constantly surrounded by armed soldiers, often of the roughest sort, she must have felt safer in her male clothing, the symbol of her promise to her Voices that she would keep her virginity 'for as long as it should please God'. She would find it hard to believe that her mission was at an end and thoughts of escape or rescue from her captors must always have been in the forefront of her mind. Almost to the end, it was her persistent and finally pathetic refusal to wear women's dress that would enable the judges at her trial to level one of the main charges against her: that of 'wearing dissolute and dishonest dress, contrary to natural decency'.

In the middle of November the faculty of the University of Paris sent a letter 'to the Most Excellent Prince, the King of France and of England', demanding that Joan be handed over to them in Paris, 'to be tried for heresy by Pierre Cauchon, Bishop of Beauvais, and by the Inquisitor of France'. This request was denied, as the English were determined to keep Joan for themselves and had already decided that she would stand trial in Rouen, a stronghold of England for over ten years.

The Final Journey

At this point, the young King Henry was living in Rouen with his guardian, Richard Beauchamp, Earl of Warwick, and had been brought over from England with the intention of having him crowned King of France. The ceremony did, in fact, take place but not until December 1431, in Paris, and proved to be a futile ploy, as by that time the majority of the French people had accepted Charles as their true and rightful King, as he had been crowned and anointed at Reims, in the cathedral that had witnessed the sacring of all the French kings, from the time of Clovis, the first Christian King of the Franks.

Because Joan had been taken prisoner at Compiègne, which was in the diocese of Beauvais, it had been agreed that Cauchon, as its Bishop, should act as judge at her trial. But under Church law, Cauchon had no rights to officiate in Rouen. The problem was, however, quickly solved by the Duke of Bedford, who persuaded the ecclesiastical authorities in Rouen to grant Cauchon a 'commission of territory', thereby giving him the right to act in that locality.

From Arras, Joan began the last five to six weeks of her journey, travelling west to the château of Le Crotoy on the estuary of the Somme. During the journey to Le Crotoy a number of stops were made, notably at Drugy, where it is on record that Joan was paid a visit by the monks of the nearby abbey of Saint-Riquier, and was allowed to hear Mass and receive Holy Communion.

The château of Le Crotoy, under English rule since 1424, was situated at the tip of a peninsula looking out over the widest part of the estuary. Here, Joan was imprisoned in the Tour du Roi, where she was visited by a number of townswomen, who came by boat from Abbeville, in those days a seaport, before the silting-up of the estuary. To be granted permission to see the famous prisoner, these ladies must have been of high rank, but whether they were drawn by curiosity or sympathy for Joan's plight is not known. Also during her stay at Le Crotoy, the Chancellor of Amiens Cathedral, Nicholas de Quiefdeville, came to see her and she was again able to receive the Sacrament so dear to her heart. But her circumstances were about to become even more harsh, and this was probably the last time she would be allowed to receive this benediction until the day of her martyrdom.

On 6 December the ransom money for Joan's sale to the English was delivered to Jean de Luxembourg, for which he gave his receipt: '10,000 *livres* for Joan, who is called the Maid, a prisoner of war'.

Meanwhile, the ever active Cauchon had a meeting in Amiens with, amongst other English commanders, William de la Pole, Earl of Suffolk, another of Joan's sworn enemies, who had played a major role in the siege of Orléans. When Joan arrived to relieve the city, he had been forced to retreat to Jargeau, where he was captured and had to pay a huge ransom for his release. The purpose of the meeting was to discuss Joan's transfer from Burgundian to English hands.

Determined to keep Joan in his sights, Cauchon accompanied the final stage of the journey to Rouen, which began on 20 December. Joan was taken with a small company by boat across the Somme to Saint-Valéry, while the main body of mounted guards left to cross the river by the bridge at Abbeville. Thereafter, the whole party, consisting of some 50 men-at-arms, travelled on via the town of Eu and followed the old Roman road through Arques and Bosc-le-Hard, arriving at the château of Bouvreuil on the outskirts of Rouen on Christmas Eve.

11   Imprisonment

Joan was imprisoned in the great château-fortress of Bouvreuil, built by King Philippe-Auguste at the beginning of the thirteenth century. Her cell was situated at the base of a tower—ever afterwards known as the Tour de la Pucelle—the remains of which can still be seen today, and may be visited in the inner courtyard of 102 rue Jeanne d'Arc. The cell was hexagonal, measuring almost six metres from wall to wall, and contained a latrine and a well. Joan's bed would almost certainly have been the only item of furnishing. In the dark and dank interior one can still poignantly experience the desolate and forbidding atmosphere of the place where she was held for the five months of life which remained to her.

During the day, Joan was fettered with leg irons, which made it extremely difficult to walk, and she had to be assisted the considerable distances to the places of her appearances before the tribunal of her judges. At night she was totally unable to move, being chained to her bed with the leg irons, which were fastened by two more chains attached to the foot of the bed, which was in turn attached to a large piece of wood, some five or six feet long.

From the start, Joan complained bitterly to Cauchon about her treatment but to no avail. It was not only the physical suffering that she had to endure; Cauchon had enlisted three Englishmen in the service of King Henry, and had them swear on the Bible to guard her with the utmost vigilance and let no one visit her who was not authorized by him. These three, whose names have survived in the records, were John Grey, a royal squire, and his assistants, John Berwoit and William Talbot. But Joan's immediate guards, who were to cause her great physical humiliation and mental torture, were five men of the lowest kind, known as *houssepailliers* (roughnecks). Three of these men spent the night inside Joan's cell, the other two standing guard outside the door. One can imagine the obscene behaviour of these men, about whom Joan constantly complained to Cauchon that, on more than one occasion, they had attempted to violate her.

At the beginning of January, Joan had to undergo another test of virginity, to which she reluctantly agreed, 'provided it is done by decent women'. The examination was supervised by Anne of Burgundy, Duchess of Bedford. One of the trial witnesses later testified that the Duke of Bedford 'stood in a hidden place, from where he could see Joan examined'. The result of the examination was the same as at Poitiers, and Joan's virginity was declared intact. The Duchess has also gone on record as forbidding Joan's guards and others 'to offer her any violence'. That Joan's virginity was still intact must have greatly displeased Cauchon, as one of the charges he wished to bring against her, that of witchcraft, could not be brought against a virgin. The result of the examination was never entered in the records of the trial.

Cauchon, meanwhile, had been busy trying to discover other grounds whereby he could implicate Joan. In December he had dispatched one of his agents to Domremy with the purpose of gaining information about her childhood and youth, the usual procedure before an inquisitorial court could proceed. It was his hope that something could be found with which to further incriminate her. Together with two local officials, the agent questioned clergy and residents in Domremy, Vaucouleurs and Toul. He returned to Rouen in January to report that nothing had been found against Joan's character. He was also quoted later by a man who had met him during the inquiry, as having said that 'he had found nothing concerning Joan which he would not have liked to find about his own sister'. Cauchon was so incensed at this news that he accused the man of lying and failing in his duty, and refused to pay him for his services. Although this appeared to be a setback for Cauchon, it would not prevent him from fabricating evidence against Joan in this respect, as well as in the matter of her virginity, during the course of the trial.

The circumstances under which Joan was held prisoner were totally unlawful, as under the accepted procedure in a trial for heresy she should have been kept in an ecclesiastical prison, guarded by women; instead, she was being treated as a prisoner of war. In order to ward off any criticism regarding this illegality, Cauchon decided on a devious plan which he hoped would demonstrate that Joan was being held entirely under the jurisdiction of the Church authorities. He had three keys made for her cell and let it be known that only those in holy orders were to be allowed access to her. One key was to be kept by

Cardinal Henry Beaufort, Bishop of Winchester, who would be present throughout the trial, and the others would be held by the judges: Cauchon himself, Jean d'Estivet, the promoter or prosecutor, and the Vice-Inquisitor.

This latter, chosen by Jean Graverent, Inquisitor of France, was Jean Lemaître, a Dominican friar of the convent in Rouen. Lemaître at first refused to take part in the proceedings, citing amongst other matters that he could not take part in the trial 'for the serenity of his conscience'. It was only after Cauchon had demanded his presence, by appealing to the Inquisitor, that he was made to attend. Although he and Cauchon were jointly judges, Lemaître would stay mostly in the background, making only rare appearances in the courtroom—it may be that he continued to sustain doubts about the validity of the proceedings. Cauchon was to be, in effect, the sole judge.

Lemaître would not be the last cleric to have serious doubts about the validity of the trial, and Cauchon would have to threaten and even imprison those who dared to oppose him. One senior figure, Jean de Saint-Avrit, Bishop of Avranches, expressed his doubts by quoting St Thomas Aquinas, 'that in matters which touch the Faith, recourse should always be had either to the Pope or to a Synod'. Only his high office saved him from Cauchon's wrath.

Of the major figures involved in the trial, there exists a damning indictment from one who was present throughout as an assessor. He was Isambard de la Pierre, a Dominican friar of the convent of Saint-Jacques in Rouen. One of the few who dared to express sympathy for Joan's plight, he would sometimes try to give her counsel and guidance, for which he was more that once threatened with his life, by both Cauchon and by the English. In his testimony for the Trial of Rehabilitation, he stated:

> Some of those who took part in the trial were, like the Bishop of Beauvais, motivated by their partiality. Others, like certain of the English, by a desire for vengeance. Others, the Paris doctors, by the lure of gain. Still others were driven by fear, like the Vice-Inquisitor, and others I do not remember; and everything was done on the initiative of the King of England, the Cardinal of Winchester, the Earl of Warwick, and other Englishmen who paid the

expenses incurred in staging this trial . . . it is my belief and judgment that the English acted against Joan out of hatred and malice, and that they had no other purpose than her death.

One hundred and seventy clergy and other officials were summoned to attend the trial. Their number included 60 assessors, or advisers, experts in theology and Church law, whose duty was to ensure that the strict rules governing a trial for heresy were followed. The judges would consult the assessors before decisions were taken against the accused. This body of men consisted of bishops, canons, doctors and bachelors of theology, doctors of medicine, Dominican priests and others. Among their number was a contingent from the University of Paris.

These highly learned men would, for the most part, try their best to ensure that the correct procedures were followed, but they would have to contend with Cauchon's frequent attempts throughout the proceedings to question their deliberations on important points, in opposition to his determination to conduct the case as he alone thought fit—although, as the trial progressed, even he would find himself under tremendous political pressure from the English lords present, notably the Cardinal of Winchester and the Earl of Warwick.

★   ★   ★

Of the prevailing religious atmosphere in the fifteenth century, and in order to gain a deeper understanding of the intrinsic nature of these churchmen preparing to sit in judgment on Joan—men who believed themselves to be true Christians—Rudolf Steiner had this to say:

> We must be quite clear in our understanding as to the difference between the continuous development of peoples and the continuous development of single human individualities.
>
> What did the people of that day understand of the Christ Impulse? The people around the Maid of Orléans called themselves 'Christians'. They understood something by their 'Christianity'. But as regards what they understood we must say: 'He whom you seek is not here; and Him who is here you have not sought, nor do you know Him.' Souls adhered to Christianity in the outer form, they wore it as a garment, in their etheric bodies and not in their astral

body. They were Christians in their waking condition, but they could not take Christianity with them when they were outside the physical and etheric body. And the great difference between the Maid of Orléans and the others was that she took in the Christ Impulse into the depths of her astral body and worked for the Christ Impulse with the profoundest forces of the astral body.

... theologians were to be found attacking all kinds of points of religion—fighting amongst themselves, and asserting themselves to be the faithful and their opponents the opposite. We see a Christian doctrine spreading abroad according to the standard of that time. But when Christ intervenes in the evolution of humanity through His servants, and working through the Maid of Orléans by means of His Michael Spirit, He intervenes as a Living Being—not merely through what man understands of Him.

If Christ had only been able to work through that which men have understood of Him He would not have been able to do much. But it is not a question of what man took in through his human understanding or of what he was able to conceive of the Christ, but of the fact that since the Mystery of Golgotha Christ is present, actually operative among men and taking part in their proceedings. It is not a question of how far He is 'understood' by men, but that He was present as a Living Being and allowed Himself to permeate all the decisive facts of evolution. When certain facts must enter into evolution for the proper progress of mankind, He Himself leads His spiritual servants.

★   ★   ★

The final arrangements were now in place for the trial which has come to be recognized as one of the most infamous in all of history. In the early years of the last century, when there was a tremendous upsurge of interest in Joan, a distinguished Scottish judge, Sir John Macdonell, in his *Historical Trials*, made a thorough study and assessment of Joan's trial, and condemned it as 'the scandal and reproach of medieval criminal law'.

Three days after Joan's nineteenth birthday on 6 January 1431, her long, agonizing months of suffering would begin. Standing before the formidable array of churchmen, and without advocate or witnesses to speak on her behalf, she was to endure relentless and intimidating interrogation, conducted from the start—as the surviving records make all too clear—to find her guilty of the charges levelled against her, of sorcery and heresy.

Joan would bear herself with great fortitude throughout the trial; her character and indomitable courage were recognized by Macdonell as 'one of those rare unions of strength, heroism and sanity, with mysticism, sagacity and grasp of facts. Her life in the invisible world did not blind her practical wisdom, conspicuous in the strange atmosphere of Courts...'

12   The Trial: Part One

Joan of Arc had been a prisoner of war for eight months, when the proceedings for her long and arduous trial began on 9 January 1431. As a prisoner of the Inquisition, what she would endure for the next five months was chillingly summarized, again by Macdonell, in his description of the inquisitorial process:

> ...a terribly potent machine, one unsurpassed in efficacy for turning innocence into guilt: one by which all securities for fair play were removed; a system under which even when physical torture was not resorted to, the accused was by repeated examination, by threats, by tricks and devices, by false suggestions, by banishing all counsel or friends, and by lowering the diet, reduced to a condition in which the prosecutor wrung out of his victim what he desired.

Forefront in the minds of those churchmen sitting in judgment on Joan were the rules governing trials for witchcraft and sorcery, the basis for which had been laid down in the thirteenth century by St Thomas Aquinas in his *Summa Theologiae* and other works, which had been taught in the universities for a century and a half.

Before the first part of the trial, the Preparatory Interrogation, could begin, certain inquiries which had been carried out were presented to the court. As previously mentioned, the first of these was the deputation to Domremy to investigate Joan's childhood and interrogate witnesses in the area who had known her; the second was her recent virginity test. In the first instance, nothing to her detriment had been discovered and, in the second, her virginity was found to be intact. The outcome, therefore, was that there were no grounds with which to formulate any charges against her. These facts were not included in the records of the trial, and it was not until the Trial of Rehabilitation that some of those who had been involved in that inquiry at Domremy, as well as witnesses to the examination for virginity, came forward and made their involvement known.

It would soon become apparent, as the trial progressed, that it was solely on the basis of Joan's own words, as they would be interpreted by her judges, that she could be tried; her absolute honesty and sincerity regarding her Voices, her belief in her mission, and her resolute refusal to compromise would give her judges every opportunity to falsify and distort her responses, and by resorting to such trickery would find the means whereby they would be able to condemn her.

On Wednesday, 21 February, when the Preparatory Interrogation began, Joan was led from her cell at 8 o'clock in the morning by Jean Massieu, the court usher, to the Chapel Royal of the château, where the first session was to take place. Wearing her chains, she was motioned by Cauchon to be seated on a small stool, facing her accusers. She must have presented a pitiful sight, pale and drawn from her months of imprisonment, her black doublet and hose by this time dirty and torn.

Before the imposing tribunal of 44 assessors, Cauchon began by asking Joan to swear to tell the truth on everything she would be asked, which she refused to do, saying, 'I do not know what you wish to ask me; perhaps you will ask things that I will not tell you.' Cauchon then became more insistent and asked her to swear to tell the truth on everything concerning the Catholic faith and anything else she knew. But Joan was adamant:

> Of my father and my mother, and all that I have done since I came into France, I will willingly swear, but of the revelations made to me by God, I have not told nor revealed to anyone, save only to Charles, my King, nor shall I reveal them though it cost me my head. I know from my visions that I must keep them secret.

At Cauchon's further insistence, Joan finally agreed to take the oath, but only on matters concerning the faith.

After this, when Joan complained about her degrading treatment at the hands of her guards, and of being kept in chains, Cauchon replied that it was necessary to keep her thus secured, in order to prevent her escape. When Joan informed him that it was her right as a prisoner of war to try to escape, Cauchon's response was to bring into court the three senior English gaolers and have them take the oath to guard her with even greater vigilance.

Cauchon then asked Joan to recite the Paternoster and Ave Maria, but she refused, 'unless you hear my confession', which put him in a very difficult situation; his duties as a priest obliged him to hear her, but her confidences would have conflicted with his position as her judge. He evaded Joan's request, and it is recorded that he tried instead to 'several times' admonish her; but she resolutely refused to recite the prayers, and with the situation in stalemate, he was finally obliged to drop the matter. At this point, the first session came to a close.

Guillaume Manchon, the court's chief notary, spoke about the nature of the trial in his testimony for the Rehabilitation, stating that, on the first day 'there was great turmoil in the chapel, when Joan was constantly interrupted when she spoke'. Massieu also testified that before she could answer on a particular point, another assessor would interject with another question, causing Joan such confusion that she frequently had to ask them to put their questions one at a time. This was a situation which would be repeated throughout the trial. Manchon also testified about the way in which attempts would be made by the assessors to trick Joan with difficult and subtle questions, by referring back to points on which she had already answered, but she would often remind them of her previous testimony, or refer them back to Manchon for confirmation.

Manchon was thoroughly meticulous in regard to his required duties as notary. It is also to his credit that he refused to proceed with his duties if the procedures were not conducted in a proper manner, by which he meant that there were present in the court other notaries employed as representatives of the English side, who were recording Joan's testimony as they thought fit—usually to her disadvantage. His insistence that he had faithfully recorded her words again met with difficulties, as when recording the proceedings, which he wrote down in French, the judges would then have the testimony translated into Latin (the usual procedure), but would often change the meaning of his words or alter what Joan had actually said. In confronting Cauchon with his refusal to have altered what he had originally set down, the result was, as he said, that 'my lord of Beauvais was greatly enraged against me'.

Joan's torment was not only confined to the court sessions, where the relentless and debasing questioning was fired at her in attempts to wear her down. Further actions were made to humiliate her, such as that related by Massieu. When he was taking Joan from her cell to the various places of interrogation, she would pause in front of the porch leading to the chapel and ask him to allow her to say a prayer before the entrance, which he allowed her to do. On one such occasion they were dismayed by the sudden appearance of the man who had been appointed by Cauchon as prosecutor of the trial, Jean d'Estivet. This vile man was ironically nicknamed 'Master Benedicite', because of his foul and obscene language. D'Estivet placed himself between Joan and the chapel door and threatened Massieu, saying, 'Traitor, what makes you so bold as to allow this excommunicated whore to approach the church without permission? If you allow it again I will have you put in prison where you will see neither the sun nor moon for a month.' Alarmed and upset though she must have been, Joan's scathing comment to d'Estivet was, 'Is *this* the body of Jesus Christ?'

D'Estivet would continue with his verbal attacks on Joan throughout the trial. (He was no longer alive by the time of the Rehabilitation—he had been found drowned in a drain.)

Also at this point an attempt was made to try to get Joan to incriminate herself, by introducing into her cell a priest who pretended to be a fellow countryman from the Meuse. This man was Nicolas Loiseleur, one of the assessors and a long-time supporter of the English cause in France. He offered to hear Joan's confession and, having done so, pretended to have news from her home. In generally ingratiating himself with her, he tried to extract any useful information to pass on to the court. Manchon, together with his fellow notary, Boisguillaume, was instructed to listen to their conversation from an adjoining room, where there was a spyhole, in order to report what was said. Although some information was taken down by them, it is not recorded whether anything was ever learned that could be used against Joan.

On the second day of the trial, the interrogation was held in the robing chamber, a smaller room adjacent to the great hall, when Cauchon again tried to make Joan take the oath, this time in a more extended form than on the previous day. To this Joan replied, 'You asked me yesterday, that should be enough. You burden me too much.'

This session was conducted by Jean Beaupère, one of the assessors, who had been an English agent for many years, having undertaken important negotiations for the cause of England in France. Beaupère mainly questioned Joan on her Voices, her departure from Vaucouleurs and the journey to Chinon. He also exhorted her to tell the truth on everything she knew, but Joan's reply was, 'You may well ask me some things about which I shall tell you, but on others I will not answer. If you were well informed about me, you would wish I was out of your hands, for I have done nothing except by revelation.' At this point, Cauchon postponed further questioning until the following Saturday.

On Saturday, 24 February, half the session was taken up by Cauchon persistently demanding that Joan must take the oath on everything she knew. He asked her three times, but each time she stubbornly refused to swear, finally telling him, 'About some things I will tell you, but not all. I am come by God's will and have nothing to do here, and demand that I be sent back to God from whom I came.'

Beaupère was again in charge of the interrogation, and began by addressing Joan on the subject of her 'Voice'. He asked her how frequently she heard it, in what manner it came to her, and what it said. Joan replied that she had heard the Voice many times in her cell, on the previous day three times, and also that morning; she was sometimes awakened from sleep by the Voice, after she had prayed that it might help her and advise her what to do, and it had advised her to 'answer boldly'.

At this point, no doubt strengthened by this thought, Joan turned to Cauchon and said, 'You say that you are my judge; consider well what you do, for in truth I am sent from God, and you are putting yourself in great peril.' In Boisguillaume's later testimony he stated that Joan 'several times' during the session confronted Cauchon in this same way.

Beaupère then asked Joan whether the Voice was a saint, or an angel coming direct from God, to which she replied that it came from God, but she was not going to say any more about it, for fear of displeasing the Voice.

Going off at a tangent, Beaupère then directed some confusing questions regarding Joan and her relationship with the King, but she would not be drawn, and stated that in everything it was God's will as to what she was able to do, adding that if she were not in the grace of God she could do nothing.

Returning to the question of the Voice, Beaupère then asked Joan what happened when it came to her, to which she replied that the light came before the Voice, but as to what she then saw, she said, 'I am not going to tell you everything, for I have not permission ... but I do say to you that it is a beautiful voice, righteous and worthy.' When Beaupère persisted in having a description, asking, 'Has it face and eyes?' Joan replied, 'You may not know that either,' adding, somewhat pointedly, 'There is a saying among little children that people are often hanged for telling the truth.'

Beaupère then returned to her statement about being able to act only if she were in the grace of God, and asked her, 'Do you know if you are in the grace of God?' This cunning question, which was intended to trap Joan, would have been impossible to answer, even by someone well versed in theology. To not be in a state of grace was to be in mortal sin; but because grace is the gift of God, no one can say that one is in possession of it. Had Joan said yes, she would have committed herself to heresy and presumption. Her sublime and immortal answer was, 'If I am not, may God put me there; if I am, may He keep me there.' In his testimony, Boisguillaume stated, 'Those who were interrogating her were stupefied.'

When the excitement caused by Joan's answer had died down, Beaupère moved on to her childhood and questioned her mainly about the Fairies' or Ladies' Tree, with its so-called magical powers of healing. Joan's answer was that she had sometimes sung and danced there with the other village children and had made garlands with which to decorate the tree on feast days, but, as far as she knew, she had never seen a fairy there or anywhere else. She also spoke of the wood called the Bois Chenu, but said she never believed in the prophecy that from there a Maid would come, who would perform marvellous acts.

Finally that day, Joan was asked if she would like a woman's dress, to which she replied, 'If you give me one I will take it and go away; otherwise I am content with this one, since it is God's will that I wear it.'

On the morning of Tuesday, 27 February, Cauchon again had his usual difficulty in trying to get Joan to take the oath, to which she now replied, 'It seems to me you ought to be satisfied; I have sworn enough.' Beaupère, who was once more in charge of the interrogation, then asked Joan how she had been since the previous Saturday. She answered, apparently somewhat wearily, 'You can see that I am as well as I can be.' However, her bearing was as always, resolute, and her humour throughout, her occasional flashes of wit and, sometimes, the sarcasm with which she made her replies would prove to be a constant frustration to the court.

* * *

Of the many thousands of books on the life of Joan of Arc, a considerable number have been devoted exclusively to the trial itself. Based on the huge mass of surviving documents, many of these are lengthy volumes, and cover the trial interrogations word for word on a daily basis. In works of a more general nature, the usual practice has been to select the main points of the trial proceedings and set them down in chronological order. From 27 February onwards the relentless questioning of Joan on every aspect of her life and mission continued, with the assessors returning time after time to the same subjects on which she had already answered. In order to avoid the repetitive nature of these sessions, the main points on which Joan was interrogated have been arranged thematically, and treated as forming part of a single session.

* * *

St Michael

The incessant probing into the nature of the 'Voices'—St Michael, and Sts Catherine and Margaret—continued. The assessors first questioned Joan on who or what she had first seen. To this she replied that it was St Michael who first appeared to her, and he was not alone, but was 'accompanied by angels from heaven'. Asked if she saw St Michael and the angels corporeally and in reality, she replied, 'I see them with my bodily eyes, as well as I am seeing you; and when they left me I wept and longed that they should take me with them.' She at first refused to tell them in what form St Michael came and what he said the first time he appeared to her, and reminded them, as she frequently did, that they should refer to her examination at Poitiers, where she had given a full and free description. Asked if there was a light when she heard the Voice: 'There is much light everywhere,' she added, pointedly, 'Not all light comes only for you.' Asked if St Michael were naked—an attempt to trick her into having witnessed a diabolic form—she replied, 'Do you think that Our Lord has not the wherewithal to clothe him?' Asked if he had hair: 'Why should it have been cut off?'

★ ★ ★

Sometimes when Joan was being interrogated, she would turn defiantly on her judges with statements imparted to her, as she said, by revelations from her Voices. On one occasion, which related to present and future events between England and France, she told Cauchon that 'many English will be stricken to the ground before the Feast of St Martin in the winter'. Seven months later on 25 October, the siege of Compiègne was raised. She also informed Cauchon that 'before seven years are passed, the English will have a greater loss than they had at Orléans ... and will suffer a greater battle than they ever had in France, and this will be by a great victory which God will send to France'. These prophetic words were realized in April 1436, when the Constable of France, Arthur de Richemont, successfully liberated Paris from English rule. Among those who hastily fled the city was Pierre Cauchon—ousted yet again from what he had thought was a safe haven. The reaction of the court to Joan's revelatory statements is not recorded.

★ ★ ★

Sts Catherine and Margaret

Information was only gradually drawn from Joan regarding the two saints. Asked how she knew they came from God, and that they were indeed the two named saints, she replied that she had told the court often enough: 'Believe me if you will.' She had previously testified that she knew the saints by the greeting each gave her, and that they told her their names. When asked if she called them or if they came without being called, she replied that they often came without being called, but '... if they do not come soon, I ask Our Lord to send them'. When asked about their appearance, she replied that she always saw them in the same form, that she saw their faces, and 'their heads are richly crowned'. To the question, 'Had they hair?', her ironic reply was, '*C'est bon a savoir!*'—'It's good to know!', implying 'Wouldn't you like to know more!'—an evasive response she often used during the trial.

On further probing about how the saints spoke to her, she replied that their voices were 'lovely, sweet and low in tone, and they spoke most excellently and beautifully in French', and she understood them perfectly. When asked if St Margaret spoke in the English tongue, Joan's quick retort was, 'Why should she speak English, when she is not on the side of the English?' Do the saints hate the English? 'They love what Our Lord loves and hate what God hates'—another trap Joan adroitly evaded. She also made the point that each in turn heard her confession—something Cauchon was no doubt extremely displeased to hear, in view of the difficulties he had experienced with her over this very problematical aspect of their relationship earlier in the trial.

Questioned about how the saints addressed her, she said, 'Every day, when they speak to me, they have called me Joan the Maid, Daughter of God.' Do you make them a reverence by bending the knee and bowing? 'Yes, and as much as I could . . . for I know well that they are those of the kingdom of Paradise.' Did she kiss and embrace them? She replied that she had embraced them both and, further, they had a delightful odour. Did she embrace the upper or the lower part? 'It is more fitting to embrace them by the lower part than the higher.' Interestingly, Joan added at this point that angels often come to Christians who do not see them, and she had often seen them among Christian folk.

★ ★ ★

Joan's ring

The question of Joan's ring arose during these interrogations. Though not in itself of great value, it had been given to her by her parents, possibly when they met at Reims for the coronation. It bore the inscription 'Jhesus-Maria', together with three crosses. Asked why she looked lovingly at it before going into battle, Joan replied that it was in honour of her father and mother and, most importantly, that while wearing it she had touched St Catherine.

She confronted Cauchon: 'You have my ring; give it back to me'—an appeal no doubt ignored.

* * *

From Saturday, 10 March, until the following Saturday, the interrogations were held in Joan's cell, with a small number of assessors present. This period must have been extremely fatiguing for her, as it meant that she had no opportunity for even a short walk and a change of air from her dismal surroundings. As Massieu later testified, she was kept in chains throughout the sessions. One of those present was an assessor appointed by Cauchon to interrogate Joan, named Jean de la Fontaine, who questioned her on a variety of subjects, such as her father and mother, and about leaving Domremy. To this, Joan gave one of her famous replies: 'Since it was God who commanded it, if I had had a hundred fathers and a hundred mothers, or if I had been the daughter of a king, I would have left.' He also asked her why she had been chosen, to which she replied, 'It pleased God so to do, by means of a simple maid, to drive back the King's enemies.' During the following days, de la Fontaine appears to have been fair in his methods of interrogation, but Cauchon apparently considered him to have been too helpful to Joan, and he was threatened by the Bishop and was forced to leave Rouen soon afterwards.

* * *

Joan's sword and standard
Many questions were put to Joan about her sword and standard. She said that her sword, found behind the altar at Fierbois, was greatly prized by her, because it was found in the church of St Catherine, whom she much loved. Questioned as to how her standard was made, she replied that it was on the instructions of the saints Catherine and Margaret, by God's commandment, that she, Joan, had it designed and made: 'I had made that figure of Christ and of the angels and in colours; and the saints said to me, "Take up the standard in the name of the King of Heaven." They told me to take it up boldly and that God would help me.' Asked why her standard was carried in the cathedral at Reims during the coronation, she replied, 'It had borne the burden, it was only right that it should have the honour.' Asked what she liked better, her

standard or her sword: 'I like much better, even 40 times, my standard to my sword ... I carried my standard when we went into battle, to avoid having to kill anyone. I have never killed anyone.'

★   ★   ★

The 'sign' given to the Dauphin
The meeting of Joan of Arc with the Dauphin was an event of the most tremendous significance. This weak and insecure man had to be convinced beyond all doubt that it was his destiny to be crowned King of France, as this was the vital first step towards the freeing of the country from English domination. As Rudolf Steiner pointed out, the expulsion of England from the soil of France was an essential deed, which determined not only the future destinies of the two countries involved, but had wider implications for Central European evolution and, in later centuries, further significance for western culture and development.

Upon her arrival at Chinon, Joan later said, 'I often prayed that God should send the King a sign'; the present writer believes that her prayer was answered when Charles was not only witness to but participated in a uniquely spiritual experience.

When Charles emerged from his private meeting with Joan, two men who were present at the court gave their accounts of his demeanour. Jean de Metz, Joan's faithful companion, in a conversation with Simon Charles, President of the Royal Treasury (who had arrived in Chinon a little while after Joan, and was obviously intrigued by the events taking place), told him, 'After having heard her, the King appeared radiant.' Alain Chartier, the court poet, in a letter to a foreign prince in July 1429, wrote, even more dramatically, that '... he looked as if he had been visited by the Holy Spirit'.

In attempting to explain the meaning of the 'sign', some historians and other Johannic writers have concluded that Joan was using the language of symbol: that she herself was the 'angel' and by speaking to the Dauphin about a 'crown' she somehow made him believe in her. That this explanation could have made him accept her as the saviour and deliverer of France does not seem entirely credible, in view of the extraordinary nature of their meeting and Charles' extreme sense of hopelessness at the time with regard to his future.

Another attempt to interpret the meaning of the 'sign', has been accepted by other writers, and relates to an account which emerged in the years following Charles VII's death in 1468. A close friend of the King and gentleman of his bedchamber was quoted in a chronicle of the time as having said that he had been told by the King himself that, in the time prior to Joan's arrival at Chinon, 'he found himself in such extremity that he no longer knew what to do, and thought only of saving his own life, for his enemies were closing in on him from all sides. In this mind the King went alone one morning into his oratory and prayed devoutly to Our Lord in his heart and without spoken utterance, asking humbly that if it were indeed true that he was of the blood of the noble House of France and rightful ruler of the kingdom, God would keep and defend him, or at the worst give him grace to escape without death or captivity...' Because Joan repeated this unspoken prayer to Charles, it is believed that this is what convinced him of his right to the throne.

The narrative may well be true, but that this alone would have been sufficient to make him believe in her is open to question. Charles had a secretive side to his odd and vacillating nature, and it is possible that he may have chosen not to disclose the full story of his meeting with Joan, but to keep to himself a much greater secret about other, even more extraordinary events that had taken place all those many years before in Chinon.

Biographers have been content to accept one or the other of the above accounts as the only possible solutions to the mystery of the 'sign'. But in the session of the trial of 13 March, which deals almost exclusively with the 'sign', if much of the misleading questioning directed at Joan is set aside—a subterfuge frequently employed by the assessors with the intention of confusing her—a very revealing picture relating to the 'sign' gradually begins to emerge from her testimony, a picture of events and phenomena which, because of their deeply esoteric nature, were unrecognized by Cauchon and the court at the time. Modern biographers have also failed to recognize their significance and have concluded that most of Joan's testimony was confused and does not, therefore, warrant any further scrutiny.

Rudolf Steiner has given the reason for this lack of recognition, and has said that 'people write biographies today without the faintest idea that great spiritual powers are at work in human destiny'. It is the failure to recognize the existence of these spiritual powers, which intervene for the guidance of humanity at crucial turning points in human evolution, that has also made it impossible to understand the true significance of the mission of Joan of Arc, and to decipher the many enigmatic episodes in her life, such as that of the mystery of the 'sign'.

The trial proceedings of 13 March, from which the following extracts have been taken, are contained in the Orléans Manuscript, compiled in the fifteenth century and believed by many Johannic scholars to be the most complete and accurate record of the Trial of Condemnation. The text set out below contains a compelling account of the 'sign' and of the incredible experience which gave the Dauphin absolute conviction about his future destiny.

In earlier sessions Joan had been closely questioned about the 'sign' she had given to the Dauphin, but all she would say was that she had sworn and promised to St Catherine that she would not reveal it. She had, however, reluctantly admitted that the 'sign' was an angel who had brought the Dauphin a crown, thereby assuring him that he would have the whole and entire realm of France through the help of God and her efforts.

In this session of 13 March, Joan was first questioned about the crown and of what material it was made, and she replied, 'It was of fine gold, and it was so rich that I could not describe its richness, and it signified that he should hold the realm of France.' Asked from where the angel had brought the crown, she said it had been brought from God . . . 'and there is no goldsmith in the world who could have made one so lovely and so precious'—a clear reference here by Joan that the crown did not have a physical origin, but was of a purely spiritual nature.

Joan was then asked whether the angel who brought the crown came from on high or from the earth: 'He came from on high . . . and by Our Lord's command.' (From this description, it is evident that the 'angel' was St Michael.) She then went on to say that he was accompanied by many angels, and in their midst St Catherine and St Margaret were to be seen. Describing how she had gone with the angel into the Dauphin's chapel, she said that he entered first, and 'when he came to the King [Dauphin], he did the King reverence, bowing before him', and 'he recalled the great patience he had shown in the great tribulations that had come upon him'. She then said to Charles, 'Sire, here is your sign: take it,' and 'he not only saw the sign, but received it'. Here, Joan is quite definitely stating that the Dauphin had actually participated in this vision of supernatural grace, the powerful effect of which had convinced him beyond all doubt that he was the rightful heir to the throne of France.

Joan was also asked if anyone else had seen the 'angel', to which she replied that the Archbishop of Reims, among others, had seen him, while others had seen only the 'crown'—a statement which appears to signify that the spiritual manifestation was at least made partially visible to some of those present in the great hall when Joan and St Michael passed through on their way to Charles' private chapel.

Joan had already stated in an earlier session that, following her meeting with the Dauphin, and after her departure from the château, she had heard that more than three hundred people there had seen the 'sign' and she knew that for love of her God was willing to allow them to see it. Further, she said that when the churchmen who were present had seen the 'sign', they stopped arguing against her 'because they knew they had seen an angel, and they also believed it from their learning'. Even so, it is apparent that the vision of the 'sign' which was given to so many was not a fully conscious experience, but took place in a semi-conscious, almost dreamlike state. Certainly, in the case of the churchmen, their ingrained, intellectual schooling quickly reasserted itself, as it was soon afterwards that they advised the Dauphin of their decision to send Joan to Poitiers to be examined by the learned doctors.

Joan was not interrogated further on the matter and after she had once again reminded the court that Charles had believed 'from the sign of the crown', this very lengthy and significant session came to an end.

★ ★ ★

Accusations of witchcraft

On several occasions attempts were made to trap Joan into admitting that her actions had been due to the practice of witchcraft. From the start, the English had denounced her as a witch, as in the accusation made by the Duke of Bedford, who had called her 'a lyme of the feende, called the Pucelle, that used fals enchauntements and sorcerie'. There was also the episode of her meeting with Brother Richard at Troyes, when he had made the sign of the cross and sprinkled holy water before her, which had brought her wry response, 'Approach boldly, I shall not fly away'—the common belief being that witches could fly through the air.

Questions about the Fairies' or Ladies' Tree near Domremy, where she had placed garlands, and around which she had innocently danced with the other village girls, were phrased in such a way as to imply that she had conjured up the fairy creatures who supposedly dwelt there, by means of spells. To this, she answered that, although one of her godmothers, Jeanne Aubry, the wife of the mayor of Domremy, who she said was a 'sensible and upright woman', had told her that she had seen them, she herself had never seen a fairy, as far as she knew, either at the tree or anywhere else.

Questioned about what she had done with her mandrake (a poisonous plant with supposed magical properties, whose root resembled the lower part of a man's body), she replied that she had never had one, but had heard it said that there was one near her village, but she had never seen it, and believed it was an evil and dangerous thing.

To the question, 'Who were those of your company who caught butterflies in your standard before Château-Thierry?', she replied that it was never done by her party, but that those of the other party, her enemies, had invented it. As stated earlier, this episode of the butterflies encircling Joan's standard was witnessed during one of the King's triumphal rides through the countryside after the coronation. Although there is no further information about this occurrence, it must have caused great wonder amongst those who saw it, and been widely circulated in order for the court to have had knowledge of it. But inevitably the nature of the phenomenon was distorted by Joan's accusers, the belief being that some insects were thought to be witches' familiars.

To subtly phrased questions hinting that her ring had magical powers, Joan admitted it was true that many women had touched her ring with their rings, but she did not know their thoughts or intentions.

Regarding the apparent restoring to life of the dead baby at Lagny, Joan said she had prayed with the women of the town before the statue of Our Lady that it might live. Questioned further if it were true that it was said to have been revived by her intercession, she simply replied, 'I never enquired.'

This line of interrogation produced nothing the assessors could use against Joan, and the whole issue of witchcraft had to be dropped fairly early on in the Trial.

★   ★   ★

The 'great victory'

Joan's daily communion with the saints Catherine and Margaret was, as she told her judges, the only consolation during her imprisonment: 'I would be dead if it were not for the revelation which comforts me each day.' When the daily interrogations became unbearable, she would often ask the court for leave to consult the saints for their advice as to how she should answer her accusers.

Almost from the start of the trial, on 1 March, the judges began an obsessive interrogation by which they hoped to learn the details of what passed between Joan and the saints, especially in relation to what promises they had made to her regarding her present situation. She at first refused to answer, except to say that they had promised to bring her to Paradise, as she had asked them. Asked whether they had made her other promises, she said they had, but she would not reveal them, but added, somewhat enigmatically, that within three months she would reveal another promise. Then asked if the saints had told her that she would be freed from prison within three months she replied that she did not know when she would be freed and, obviously irritated by the probing, added defiantly, 'those who wish to remove me from this world might well themselves go first'. The judges persisted in this line of questioning, but all she would say was, 'Ask me in three months' time, and I will then give you my reply.'

Joan was asked several times if she would attempt to escape, the first time when she complained about being fettered with leg irons. Her reply then was, 'It is true that formerly I tried to escape from prison, as it is the right of every prisoner to do. If I could escape, I could not be reproached with having violated my word, for I have never given it to anyone.'

Later, asked if she had leave from God or from her Voices to escape from prison whenever she pleased, Joan replied, 'I have often asked for it, but so far I have not obtained it.' Asked if she would go at once if she saw her opportunity: 'If I saw the door open and my guards and the rest of the English unable to resist, I would understand that I had permission, and that Our Lord would send me help. But without leave I would not go, unless I made a forcible attempt and so learn if Our Lord would be pleased.' She then quoted the proverb in support of this: 'Help yourself and God will help you.'

During the following days, when again asked if she knew by revelation that she would escape, she replied, 'Yes, indeed, my saints have told me that I shall be delivered, but I know neither the day nor the hour, but they have told me I must put a brave face on it. St Catherine has told me that I shall receive succour, but I know not if I shall be liberated from prison, or if, while being tried, by some disturbance I may be freed; I believe it will be one or the other. Several times my Voices have told me I should be delivered by a great victory. They have also told me to take all cheerfully and not despair on account of my martyrdom, for by it I shall come at last to the Kingdom of Paradise. This my Voices tell me will happen without fail.'

At this point Joan spoke of her martyrdom as 'the pain and suffering I am undergoing in prison, and I know not if I shall suffer greater misery, but I put all my faith in Our Lord'. She was then asked if, as her Voices had promised her that in the end she will come to the Kingdom of Heaven, she believes herself assured of salvation, and that she will not be damned in hell. She replied, 'I firmly believe what my Voices have told me, that I shall be saved, as firmly as if I were already there.' Told that this answer carried great weight, she replied, 'I, too, hold it to be a great treasure.' Questioned whether after this revelation she believes that she cannot commit mortal sin, she replied, 'I know nothing about that, but in all things I trust in Our Lord.'

From the above testimony, taken directly from the trial records, it can be seen that Joan alternated between hope when in communion with her saints and despair when subjected to the relentless interrogation by the judges. It was only towards the end that she despaired of gaining her freedom, but as the testimony clearly shows, the saints never told her that she would escape from prison; what they did promise was that she would be delivered by a 'great victory', a promise which Joan believed would be her release from captivity. Mercifully, she never realized the true significance of their words, which would have made the long months of her imprisonment impossible to bear.

The saints' guidance would continue to sustain and comfort Joan throughout the following months in her battles with the judges. But her fate had long been decided by her enemies and, almost three months to the day from the interrogation, on 1 March, the saints' promise would be fulfilled. On Wednesday, 30 March, her deliverance, her 'great victory', would be the day of her martyrdom.

★ ★ ★

The fatal charges

As all previous accusations against Joan had failed to build a foundation upon which to charge her, the court was at a total loss as to how to proceed further. The judges would eventually devise a plan to charge her on two counts: the wearing of men's clothes, and her refusal to submit to the authority of the Church. It would be Joan's persistent and unwavering refusals to submit to the judges on these two charges that would ultimately result in her condemnation.

The male attire
When asked if her Voice had told her to wear a man's dress, Joan answered that the dress was but a small matter, but 'I have not taken it by the advice of any living man, nor have I done anything at all save by the command of Our Lord and the angels'. She added later, 'Since I do so at the command of God and in His service, I do not believe that I do ill; and as soon as it shall please Him to order me, it will be left off.'

Asked later what guarantee and what succour she expected to have from Our Lord in taking man's dress, she said, 'Both in the matter of this dress and in the other things I have done, I expect nothing but the salvation of my soul.'

The woman's dress
Joan was first asked if she would wear a woman's dress, to which she replied, 'Give me one and I will take it and go away. Otherwise I will not take it. I am content with this one, since it is God's will that I wear it.' On a later occasion, arguments arose between Joan and the court when she asked to hear Mass. She was asked whether it was more proper to hear Mass in a woman's dress, and would she wear a woman's dress and hear Mass or keep her male clothing and not hear Mass. Joan then asked them to promise she could hear Mass if she changed, and was promised that she could do so, to which she agreed, but added that, when she came back from Mass, she would again put on her male clothes, as she had 'sworn and promised always to wear them'. When told she must wear a woman's dress 'unconditionally and absolutely', she appeared at first to agree, but then changed her mind and insisted on keeping her male clothes. She obviously suspected a trap and realized that if she relinquished her male attire, it would not be returned to her. When the question arose again, Joan said, 'I would rather die than go back on what Our Lord has commanded me to do,' but added that all she asked, if she were found guilty, was that she would be granted a woman's dress. Asked why, if she wears a man's dress by command, does she ask for a woman's dress in her last hours, all she would reply was, 'It suffices that it be long.'

★   ★   ★

The Church demands . . .
The court frequently demanded that Joan should submit in all matters to the authority of the Church, a charge that was often combined with the insistence that she change her male attire for a woman's dress—the ploy that was used against her to make the male attire the symbol of her refusal to submit, and by which they contrived to give an appearance of justification when it came to their final sentence against her.

At the start of every session of the trial, Joan repeatedly clashed with Cauchon about the manner of taking the oath. He wanted her to swear 'absolutely and without condition' to tell the truth about everything she would be asked, but she always refused to comply, stating similarly each time, as she had said from the start, 'By my faith, you might ask me such things as I will not tell you ... especially concerning my revelations that I have sworn not to say.'

When it came to the question of her submission to the Church, Jean de la Fontaine had asked Joan if she would abide by the Church's decision on everything she had said and done, but her reply was, 'I abide by God who sent me, by Our Lady and by all the blessed saints in Paradise. And I believe God and the Church to be the same thing, about which one should make no difficulty. Why do you make such difficulty over that?' De la Fontaine had then explained to Joan that the Church Triumphant was God, the saints, the angels and the souls already saved. Of the Church Militant, he quoted the Pope as its head and all the prelates of the Church, and all good Catholic Christians. He pointedly added that because the Church is ruled by the Holy Spirit it cannot err, therefore she should be willing to submit to the Church Militant. Joan's reply to this was, 'I went to the King of France from God and the Virgin Mary and all the saints in Paradise and the Church Triumphant on high, and by their commands. And to that Church I submit all my good deeds and all that I have done and shall do. As for submitting myself to the Church Militant, I shall make no other answer now.'

Joan was also questioned as to whether she would answer 'more fully and freely' if she were to stand before the Pope—a right of every prisoner in a Church trial. She answered, 'I demand to be taken before our Lord the Pope, and then I will answer before him all that I ought to answer.' The court, of course, had no intention of granting such a request.

★ ★ ★

On Palm Sunday, 25 March, Joan was visited in her cell by Cauchon and a number of assessors, including all the delegates from the University of Paris. She was again asked if she would put on female clothing so that she might hear Mass and receive the Eucharist at Easter, but she replied that it was impossible for her, and pleaded to be allowed to hear Mass in her male attire, adding, 'These clothes do not burden my soul, and to wear them is not against the Church.' Her request was refused.

The first part of the trial was now at an end, but as no specific charges had been found which could be brought against Joan, Cauchon and the assessors were becoming increasingly frustrated as to how they could proceed against her. It was eventually decided that certain charges would be formulated, based on their interrogations since the start of the trial in February. These would be known as the Seventy Articles of Accusation, and would be placed before Joan when the second part of the trial began.

13   The Trial: Part Two

On Monday, 26 March, the second phase of the trial, the Trial in Ordinary, began, with the prosecutor, Jean d'Estivet, reading the Seventy Articles of Accusation to the court. The reading occupied the whole day and the next and stated the main points of the previous interrogations, but without including any of Joan's replies. Joan interrupted at the end of almost every clause, by denying what was stated or by referring the prosecutor to what she had said at the time.

On Wednesday, 28 March, she was again questioned about her saints, and again refused to answer certain questions, but stated that they were indeed St Michael, St Gabriel (the first time this saint is mentioned by her), St Catherine and St Margaret, 'whom Our Lord sends to comfort and guide me', adding, 'I will call them to my aid as long as I live'. When asked how she called them, she replied with a prayer which the notaries never converted into Latin, but left in French, as Joan said it: 'Most sweet Lord, in honour of Your Holy Passion, I beseech You, if You love me, to reveal unto me what I should answer to these churchmen. I well know, as to my dress, by whose command I took it, but I know not how I should leave it off; wherefore, may it please You to inform me. And they come immediately.'

By Joan's refusal to submit to the Church Militant, Cauchon had decided that he had grounds for a valid accusation against her and, on Saturday, 31 March, she was again asked to submit to the judgment of the Church. Her reply was that she would abide by the Church Militant, provided it did not command anything impossible, which she defined as having to 'revoke the deeds ... concerning the visions and apparitions sent to me by God; I shall not revoke them for anything whatsoever; that which Our Lord has made me do and commanded and will command I shall not fail to do for any man alive, and in the case of the Church willing me to do otherwise and contrary to the commandment which has been given to me by God I should not do it for anything whatsoever.' Questioned as to what she would do if the Church Militant told her that her revelations were 'illusions and things diabolical', would she then submit to the Church's decision, she again repeated that she would submit, but 'I will always abide by God whose commandment I have always done... And in the case of the Church Militant commanding me to do the contrary, I should not abide by any man in the world but only by Our Lord whose good commandment I have always done.' Finally, when asked if her Voices had commanded her not to submit to the Church Militant, nor to its judgment, she replied, 'they do not command me that I obey not the Church, Our Lord being first served'.

The Seventy Articles of Accusation may have been thought to be too rambling and not precise enough to accuse Joan, and the decision was taken by some of the assessors and some from the University of Paris to reduce the Accusations to twelve short and more specific Articles. At the Trial of Rehabilitation the chief notary, Guillaume Manchon, stated that he had not drawn up the new Articles and believed that the principal points had been summarized in order to present the matter briefly and to hasten the court's deliberations. He also stated that he had noticed at the time that, apart from other inconsistencies, certain of the Articles expressed the very opposite of what Joan had answered, and although he and the other notaries also testified that they had seen the Articles, they were not allowed to give any opinion as to their fairness to Joan, and that she never saw them.

Various deliberations were carried out in April, and some of the University of Paris clerics drew up a letter accusing Joan of false revelations and of being guilty of 'idolatry, schism, heresy, blasphemy and vaingloriousness'. Cauchon placed this letter with the twelve Articles and presented them to the assessors on 5 April, who were instructed to send in their opinions in writing by 10 April, but only a few responded. On 13 April, the Articles were taken to Paris by Jean Beaupère and others for consideration by the University.

Of the assessors consulted, many had not regularly attended the first part of the trial and could only give their opinion from the Articles. Others had been chosen by Cauchon for their devotion to the English cause and were, therefore, easy to convince. There were, however, others who were not happy with the way in which the trial was proceeding, and Cauchon encountered some resistance from these clergy, many of whom were of high rank in the Church. The Bishop of Avranches, Jean de Saint-Avit, voiced his concerns, stating that, when doubt arose in matters concerning the Faith, he held to the opinion of St Thomas Aquinas, that recourse should be made to the Pope and the General Synod. His high office saved him from Cauchon's wrath at the time, but in the following year he would be accused of involvement in a plot to liberate Rouen and, in spite of his great age, was thrown into prison.

Two clerics who dared to oppose Cauchon were Jean Lohier, a priest visiting Rouen at the time, and an assessor, Nicolas de Houppeville, a University of Paris doctor of theology. Lohier declared the trial proceedings to be 'worthless' and, in a conversation with Manchon, told him that he thought the trial was only being conducted out of hatred for Joan. When Cauchon heard of this he was so furious that Lohier immediately left Rouen for Rome, where he resided permanently. De Houppeville testified at the Rehabilitation that, because he had declared the case against Joan to be unfair and one-sided 'for many reasons', Cauchon ordered his imprisonment, and it was only by the intervention of a higher Church authority that he was eventually released.

Whilst all this dissension continued during April between Cauchon and the various clergy, Joan was suddenly taken ill. Jean Tiphaine, the Duchess of Bedford's physician, gave a detailed account of this time for the Trial of Rehabilitation. He stated that he was called to attend Joan, with, amongst others, Guillaume de la Chambre, Master of Medicine, and that they were all taken to Joan's cell by the vile Jean d'Estivet. After taking Joan's pulse, Tiphaine asked her where she felt pain, and she replied that she had eaten a carp sent to her by Cauchon, which had made her ill. At this point, d'Estivet interrupted him and accused Joan, saying, 'It is you, wanton, who has eaten shad and other things that have made you sick.' When Joan answered that she had not, a fierce argument arose between them, with many insulting words exchanged.

De la Chambre also gave evidence for the Trial of Rehabilitation, and stated that he had been sent to attend Joan by the Earl of Warwick and by Cardinal Beaufort, Bishop of Winchester. He said that Warwick had told him to take great care of Joan, as not for anything in the world would she be allowed to die a natural death, as the King [Henry

VI] had bought her dear and would not have her die excepting at the hands of justice, and that she be burnt. When Joan was found to be feverish, de la Chambre and the others decided to bleed her and, upon reporting this to Warwick, they were told to do it carefully, 'for she is cunning and might kill herself'. After she was bled, Joan recovered, but d'Estivet again arrived on the scene and began calling her 'whore and slut'. This verbal assault so upset Joan that she became ill again. When Warwick heard of this, he ordered d'Estivet to stop his insulting behaviour towards her.

On Wednesday, 18 April, Joan was not fully recovered and still confined to her bed, but it was decided to administer the first Charitable Admonition, the purpose of which was to ask for submission to the Church. Cauchon entered her cell with several others, including the Vice-Inquisitor, Jean Lemaître, and three of the clergy from the University of Paris. Cauchon informed Joan that she must decide to take counsel from among the assessors, and if she refused she would be in great danger. Joan replied, 'It seems to me, in view of the sickness that I have, that I am in great danger of death, and if such is God's pleasure for me, I ask to make confession and receive the sacrament of the Eucharist, and be buried in consecrated ground.' Some debate followed between Joan and Cauchon regarding her submission, but she was adamant, as before.

A second Charitable Admonition took place on 2 May during which Cauchon was absent on other business. Jean de la Fontaine, assisted by Isambart de la Pierre and Martin Ladvenu, again read the charges to Joan, who appears to have been fully recovered from her illness. Again warned that she must submit, she readily agreed to do so, but added, 'I believe in the Church on earth; but for my deeds and words, as I have previously said, I refer the whole matter to God, who caused me to do what I have done.' After further debate, when asked if she would submit to the Pope, she replied, 'Take me to him and I will answer him.' When Cauchon returned, and upon hearing of Joan's reply, he demanded to know who had been advising her. When told it was de la Fontaine, he became angry with Jean Lemaître for allowing de la Fontaine to conduct the session in that manner, and threatened such dire consequences that de la Fontaine, hearing of this, left Rouen for good. The two religions, de la Pierre and Ladvenu, were only saved from Cauchon's wrath by Lemaître insisting that, if they were punished, he would refuse to take any further part in the trial.

In subsequent sessions the question of submission to the Church came up repeatedly. Joan was told that if she did not submit she would be declared a heretic and could be punished 'with the pain of fire'. Her reply at one point was, 'If I saw the fire, I should still say all that I am saying.' Attempts were made to make Joan agree that the proceedings of the trial should be sent to the Pope, that he might judge them, but she was wary, and told Cauchon that this was not satisfactory, as she did not know what the proceedings would say. She insisted that Cauchon and all the court were her mortal enemies. Cauchon, becoming ever more frustrated, forbade Manchon to enter her submission to the Pope in the records, which prompted Joan to say, 'Ah, you take care to write down what is against me, and will not write down what is for me.'

It was next decided to threaten Joan with torture, and on Wednesday, 9 May, she was taken to the dungeon in the Great Tower of the château, where she was again told that she must tell the truth on all matters on which she had previously been questioned. Her response was: 'Truly, if you were to have my limbs torn off and send the soul out of my body, I should not say otherwise; and if I did say otherwise, I should afterwards say that you had made me say so by force.' She then added, 'At the last feast of the Holy Cross' (which had taken place on 3 May) 'I had comfort from St Gabriel, and I believe that it was he, and I learned it from my Voices that it was St Gabriel. I asked counsel of my Voices if I should submit myself to the Church, since churchmen were pressing me hard to submit ... and these Voices told me that if I wanted God to help me I must trust in Him for all I did. I know well that God has been the master of all that I have done, and that the devil has never had power over my deeds. I have asked my Voices whether I shall be burnt and they have answered me that I should trust in Our Lord and that He would help me.'

The executioner, Maugier Leparmentier, who was called with his assistants to administer the torture, testified at the Trial of Rehabilitation that she answered her questioners 'with such prudence that those who were there marvelled, and I retired without doing anything'. On Saturday, 12 May, Cauchon assembled twelve assessors to discuss whether Joan should again be threatened with the torture, but only three agreed and the whole matter was dropped.

Richard Beauchamp, Earl of Warwick and Governor of Rouen, gave a lavish banquet on Sunday, 13 May, to which many high-ranking persons were invited. Amongst the guests were some directly connected with Joan: Pierre Cauchon and Jean de Luxembourg, Joan's captor who had imprisoned her at Beaurevoir. Also present were Humphrey, Earl of Stafford, Constable of France for Henry VI, and Haimond de Macy, the Burgundian knight who had attempted to take liberties with Joan when she was a prisoner at Beaurevoir.

These men must have discussed Joan during the dinner and, in his statement for the Trial of Rehabilitation, de Macy testified that, late that evening, it was Luxembourg who suggested they should visit Joan in her prison. Accompanied by Warwick and Stafford, and no doubt the worse for drink, when they entered her cell Luxembourg began taunting her, saying, 'Joan, I am come to ransom you, provided you will promise never to take up arms against us again.' At this, Joan answered, 'In God's name, you are mocking me, for I know that you have neither the power nor the will to do this.' Luxembourg persisted in this vein for some time, with Joan still defying him. Finally, although almost driven to despair by this contemptible attack, she rounded defiantly on them with the words, 'I know well that these English will put me to death, because they think, after my death, to win the kingdom of France. But were they a hundred thousand *godons* (goddams: the usual English oath) more than they are now, they will not have the kingdom.' De Macy stated that, at this outburst from Joan, the Earl of Stafford became enraged, and drew his dagger to strike her, but was prevented by the Earl of Warwick. (*One defenceless girl against the flower of French and English chivalry!*)

During the banquet, Warwick had expressed his dissatisfaction to Cauchon at the slow progress of the trial. However, events began to move more quickly after Cauchon received a letter from the Faculty of the University of Paris, stating that, following their deliberations, they had found Joan to be guilty of being 'a schismatic, an apostate, a liar, a soothsayer, suspect of heresy, and of erring in the Faith and being a blasphemer of God and the saints'. This was just what Cauchon needed to hasten the proceedings and, on Saturday, 19 May, he assembled the assessors to ask for their opinions on the conclusions reached by the University. As expected, most agreed with the findings and, on Wednesday, 23 May, Joan was summoned to appear before the court.

A young Doctor of Theology, Pierre Maurice, who was also an assessor, read a lengthy dissertation to Joan, consisting of twelve Articles, each indictment reading 'You have said...', outlining all the statements which she had given during the trial, at the end of which were the words 'the clerks say...', denouncing all her words and actions. Maurice then read out a long Charitable Admonition, which began 'Joan, my very dear friend...', and ended with the words, 'I do admonish, beg and exhort you, by the pity that you feel for the Passion of Our Saviour, your Creator, and the desire you must have for the salvation of your soul and body, to correct and amend your faults and return into the way of truth, obeying and submitting yourself to the judgment and decision of the Church. And in so doing you will save your soul, and deliver, as I hope, your body from death. But if you do the contrary, and persist in your evil ways, be assured that your soul will be damned, and I fear also the destruction of your body. From which may God preserve you. Amen.'

To this, Joan gave her courageous and magnificent response: 'As for my words and deeds, I refer to what I said at my trial, and I will maintain what I have always said. And if I were to be condemned and saw the fire lit and the wood prepared and the executioner who was to burn me ready to cast me into the fire, still in the fire would I not say anything other than I have said. And I will maintain what I have said until death.'

To this reply, Manchon wrote in the margin of his notes the words—which can still be seen today in the extant record of the trial—*Responsio superba*.

14   Abjuration and Relapse

With Joan now a pronounced heretic, Cauchon lost no time in arranging a public condemnation, and chose for the site the cemetery of the abbey church of Saint-Ouen, a large open space by the church, used for various public gatherings. Here he hoped to further intimidate and humiliate Joan before the inhabitants of Rouen, who were expected to attend the scene in great numbers.

On the morning of Thursday, 24 May, Joan was taken in a cart to the cemetery and ordered to stand on a small wooden platform, one of a number erected especially for the occasion. At her side, as always, was the usher, Jean Massieu. Seated on the other platforms were Cauchon, the Vice-Inquisitor and Cardinal Henry Beaufort, together with various high church dignitaries and some 40 assessors.

A large crowd had gathered to witness the spectacle, many of whom were no doubt drawn by curiosity to see Joan for the first time. The proceedings began with a sermon, a usual part of the ceremony, which was preached by Guillaume Érard, Canon of Rouen and a member of the University of Paris, who took as his text the words from St John's Gospel, 'As the branch cannot bear fruit of itself, except it abide in the vine, no more can ye, except ye abide in Me.'

After delivering the sermon, Érard began to shout aloud about the state of France and of how it had been brought into dishonour by Charles, 'who calls himself King' and, pointing his finger at Joan, he called Charles a heretic and schismatic. Joan, unable to contain herself at this insult, cried out, 'Do not speak of my King, he is the noblest Christian of all the Christians.' At this, Érard said to Massieu, 'Make her be silent.'

Érard then turned to the question of submission to the Church, with Joan again saying, 'I abide by God and our Holy Father the Pope,' at which Érard replied that it was impossible to go to the Pope 'because of the great distance'. After repeating his demand for submission three times, and receiving no response from Joan, he directed Massieu to read her the words written on the abjuration document, a slip of parchment, later described as a short *cédule*, and consisting of a few lines in French. Massieu later testified that Joan neither understood the document nor the danger which threatened her. When he explained to her that she must sign or she would be burnt, she agreed that, if she was advised to sign by the clerics of the Church, she would abide by their decision. Érard, impatient to learn how Massieu was advising Joan, then said to her, 'Do it now, or you will go to the fire this very day.' Aware of the executioner standing nearby with his cart and waiting for her to be delivered to him, Joan replied that she would rather sign than be burnt.

At this point, the delay in getting Joan to sign was, according to Manchon's testimony, causing a 'great tumult in the crowd, and stones were thrown'. There was also confusion around Joan, with Cauchon involved in a fierce argument with Laurent Calot, Secretary to the King of England, who was accusing him of unnecessary delay and calling him 'traitor', at which insult Cauchon refused to continue unless he had an apology. Calot persisted in his attack, also charging Cauchon with being too lenient towards Joan and of betraying the English by accepting her abjuration.

Upon being ordered to sign the *cédule*, Joan was either dazed by the whole situation around her or, in spite of the pressures, still hesitating to commit herself, as she first drew a circle in place of her signature. On seeing this, Calot told her to sign properly, but again she resisted, and made a mark in the form of a cross, whilst at the same time, it was recorded, she began to laugh out loud. Although a strange thing to do under the circumstances, her laugh was obviously derisory, as a cross was the sign she had used on letters during her campaigns to warn her captains to believe the opposite of what was written, should the letters fall into enemy hands. Finally, Massieu guided her hand to write her signature, *Jehanne*.

Regarding the short *cédule* signed by Joan, Massieu later testified that he could clearly see that the paper he read to her consisted of no more than eight lines and stated that she would no longer bear arms, nor wear men's clothes, nor have her hair cut short, as well as a few other things he did not remember. What is known for certain is that the document of abjuration, which was actually entered in the trial records at the time, was a lengthy one, consisting of 47 lines and accused Joan of many crimes against the Church. This deliberate falsification would be denounced by Manchon and other witnesses at the Trial of Rehabilitation and declared by the Promoter of those proceedings as 'an abjuration artificially fabricated'.

By her abjuration, Joan had escaped the extreme penalty, as only those who had abjured and again relapsed could be sentenced to death. Cauchon had succeeded in securing the abjuration by gaining Joan's refusal to never again wear male attire, but this would not be the end of the matter—it would be the means by which he and his English masters would finally be able to trap her.

Although reformed heretics might only be sentenced to as little as three years imprisonment, Joan was about to receive a cruel blow when Cauchon pronounced the Definitive Sentence against her. He began, 'In the name of the Lord, Amen.' Citing the trial procedure and those 'by whom you have been charitably admonished with long appeals for your change of heart', he ended, 'Notwithstanding these warnings and remonstrances ... you have rashly and wantonly fallen into sin. Wherefore, that you may make salutary penance, we have condemned you ... to perpetual imprisonment, with the bread of sorrow and the water of affliction, that you may weep for your sins, and never more commit them.'

Upon leaving Saint-Ouen, one of the assessors, Nicolas Loiseleur, said to Joan that she had done well to save her soul, to which she replied, 'Come now, some of you churchmen, take me to your prison, that I shall no longer be in the hands of the English.' Manchon, who was present, later testified that Cauchon answered, 'Take her back to where you found her.' Martin Ladvenu, in his testimony, stated that, after Saint-Ouen, Cauchon asked the advice of the entire court as to whether Joan should be kept in a secular prison or in a Church prison, and although the assessors decided on the latter, Cauchon answered that he could not do that for fear of displeasing the English. By this decision Joan remained a political prisoner, entirely at the mercy of her enemies.

According to an eyewitness at the scene, as Cauchon was leaving Saint-Ouen, he was accosted by some of the English leaders who were very angry that Joan had not been condemned and delivered to them for execution, and the Bishop and the assessors were even threatened with drawn swords. The Earl of Warwick complained to Cauchon that the King had been ill-served because Joan would escape them, but Cauchon replied, 'Have no fear, my Lord, we'll catch her yet.'

Joan was taken back to her cell, where later that day she was visited by the Vice-Inquisitor and others, who warned her against relapsing into her sins and she, no doubt still extremely confused, nevertheless expressed her willingness to resume a woman's dress. Her hair, which she had previously worn *en rond*, like a soldier's, was shaved off completely.

Relapse

The last few days of Joan's life were filled with anguish and suffering. She remained guarded day and night and was constantly subjected to verbal and physical abuse by her gaolers. In her woman's dress she was even more vulnerable than before, and it was inevitable that circumstances would make it impossible for her to continue to wear it.

The reason Joan would give for resuming her male clothing was, as Isambart de la Pierre later testified, because: 'The English had had much wrong and violence done to her in prison when she was dressed in woman's clothes ... and indeed I saw her weeping, her face covered with tears, and so disfigured and outraged that I had pity and compassion on her.' Martin Ladvenu, who also gave evidence, stated: 'Someone approached her secretly at night, and I heard from Joan's own lips that a great English lord entered her cell and tried to take her by force.'

There are other explanations of the circumstances under which Joan resumed her male attire. Although she would tell the court that she had reverted to her male dress entirely of her own free will, it is possible that she realized the enormity of what she had done in disobeying the original commands of her Voices to wear male clothes. There is also the possibility that, rather than reverting to her male attire, she in fact retained it, following a major incident which occurred on the morning of Sunday, 27 May. Apparently, when Joan had been returned to prison, her male clothes had been left in a sack in her cell. According to Jean Massieu, when she awoke in the morning, she found that her guards had hidden her woman's clothes and left only the male attire. She asked the guards for her woman's dress, saying, 'Take off my irons, as I must get up.' The guards then took out the male clothing and threw it at her, saying, 'Get thyself up,' to which Joan replied, 'Gentlemen, you know it is forbidden me; without fail I will not wear it.' She continued arguing with the guards until noon, when finally, 'for the necessity of the body' she got up and had to put on the male attire. When she returned, the guards still refused to return her woman's dress, despite her repeated entreaties.

Upon hearing that Joan was again wearing her male clothes and had, therefore, relapsed, Cauchon went to her cell the next morning, accompanied by the Vice-Inquisitor and some of the assessors. After questioning her as to why she had resumed her male attire, Joan replied, 'I have done it of my own will, and because it was more fitting since I am with men. I began to wear it again because what was promised me has not been observed, to wit that I should go to Mass and receive the Body of Christ and be freed from these irons.' Cauchon then told her that when she had made her abjuration she had promised not to resume wearing man's clothes, to which she replied, 'I would rather die than remain in these irons, but if I am permitted to go to Mass and be put in a decent prison with women to help me, I will be good and do what the Church wishes.' Cauchon ignored this and asked her if, since Thursday, she had heard the voices of St Catherine and St Margaret, and she replied, 'Yes, God has sent to me by Sts Catherine and Margaret great sorrow for the mighty betrayal to which I consented in making abjuration and revocation to save my life, and that I was damning myself to save my life.' (The notary recorded in the margin of the trial records, *Responsio mortifera*—fatal answer.)

Joan went on to state that her Voices had told her, in detail, what would happen at Saint-Ouen, and how she should answer her accusers, and: 'If I were to say that God had not sent me, I should damn myself; it is true that God sent me. My Voices have since told me that I did a great injury in confessing that I had not done well in what I had done. All that I said and revoked that Thursday, I did only because of fear of the fire.'

Joan was now condemned by her own words, and Cauchon pronounced her 'heretic, obstinate and relapsed'. Isambart de la Pierre was present and said Joan answered publicly to all gathered there, 'If you, my lords of the Church, had kept and guarded me in your prisons, perhaps it would not be so with me.'

As Cauchon left Joan's cell, he met the Earl of Warwick, to whom he was heard to say, in English, 'Farewell, be of good cheer; it is done. She is caught.'

Cauchon lost no time in summoning the principal assessors to meet on the following day, in order to give their opinions on what should now be done with Joan. The first to give his opinion was Nicolas de Venderès, who had been responsible for drawing up the false abjuration document. As expected, he was emphatic that Joan should be handed over to the secular arm without delay. Giles de Duremort, Abbé of Fécamp, however, disagreed. He stated that he felt Joan, although a relapsed heretic, should have the *cédule* explained to her again. Of the 40 assessors, only two were in favour of passing sentence straight away; the rest, surprisingly, in view of their previous attitude to Joan throughout the trial, were in agreement with the Abbé, and all expressed the need to explain further to her the life and death situation with which she was faced.

Unsurprisingly, after the debate, Cauchon decided to ignore entirely the opinions of the assessors and, after thanking them, declared that 'the said Joan be proceeded against as a relapsed heretic according to law and reason'.

Later that day, all the assessors were notified that Joan, having fallen again into the errors which she had abjured, would be taken to the Vieux Marché, the Old Marketplace, in Rouen, at eight o'clock next morning to be declared 'relapsed, heretic and excommunicated'.

15   Martyrdom

At seven o'clock on the morning of Wednesday, 30 May, Martin Ladvenu, who had been chosen by Cauchon to inform Joan of her fate, visited her cell, accompanied by his assistant, Jean Toutmouillé, a young brother Dominican. As Toutmouillé later testified, Ladvenu's instructions were 'to induce in her true contrition and penitence, and to hear her confession, which he did very kindly and charitably'. But when Ladvenu began to tell her the nature of the death by which she was to die that day, she became very distressed, and cried out, 'Alas, am I to be so cruelly and horribly treated that my pure and unblemished body, which has never been corrupted, must today be consumed and reduced to ashes! Oh, I had rather be seven times beheaded than to be thus burnt. Alas, if only I had been in the prisons of the Church to which I have submitted myself and been guarded by men of the Church and not by my enemies and foes, I should not have come to this miserable end. Oh, I appeal to God, the Great Judge, to see the great wrongs and griefs that are done me.' Toutmouillé said that Joan also 'complained most bitterly about the wrongs done to her in prison by her gaolers and by others who had been let in to harm her'.

Shortly afterwards, Cauchon entered her cell and Joan confronted him directly, saying, 'Bishop, I die by you.' Cauchon tried to remonstrate with her and told her that she had to die because she had broken her promise to the Church and returned to her former sins, but Joan again insisted, 'If you had only put me in the Church court's prisons and entrusted me to decent and proper keepers, all this would never have happened. Therefore I appeal against you before God.'

Later, having heard Joan's confession, Ladvenu sent the usher, Jean Massieu to ask Cauchon if he would be allowed to give her the sacrament of the Eucharist, a rite normally forbidden to an excommunicated heretic. Following some deliberation with other officials of the court, Cauchon surprisingly agreed. When the Host was taken to Joan's cell, Massieu said it was 'without stole or candle', and he was deputed to bring them, in order that the ceremony could be properly administered. Ladvenu, in his testimony, said that Joan received the

Eucharist 'with such humility, devotion and copious tears as I could not describe'. Afterwards, when Joan asked him, 'Where shall I be tonight?', he replied, 'Have you no faith in Our Lord?,' and she answered, 'Yes, and God willing, today I shall be with Him in Paradise.'

At 9 o'clock, wearing a long robe and with her shaven head covered by a small cap, Joan was taken in a cart to the place of her martyrdom, the Vieux-Marché where, tradition has it, a crowd of ten thousand had gathered, spilling into the side streets around the marketplace. Massieu said that he and Ladvenu walked beside the cart, which was accompanied by an escort of eight hundred soldiers armed with swords and axes. Four large platforms had been erected: two for the judges and Church dignitaries, and the English lords and civil authorities of Rouen, and the third for Nicolas Midi, a Master of the University of Paris, who was to deliver the sermon. The fourth platform was made of plaster and built very high, into which the stake had been inserted and beneath which the faggots were piled.

A sign had been nailed to the stake, which read

> JEHANNE, WHO HAD CALLED HERSELF THE MAID,
> LIAR, DECEIVER OF THE PEOPLE, SORCERESS,
> BLASPHEMER OF GOD, PRESUMPTIOUS AND
> PERNICIOUS,
> DEFAMER OF THE FAITH OF JESUS CHRIST,
> BOASTFUL AND IDOLATROUS,
> CRUEL AND DISSOLUTE,
> INVOKER OF DEMONS,
> APOSTATE, SCHISMATIC AND HERETIC.

Midi's sermon, which lasted for a full hour, was based on St Paul's First Epistle to the Corinthians: 'Whether one member suffer, all members suffer with it'. Massieu said that Joan listened to the sermon 'with great fortitude and most calmly, showing signs and evidence and clear proof of her contrition, penitence and fervent faith'.

After the sermon was over, Cauchon read the Definitive Sentence, customary in trials for heresy, with its request to the secular authorities for leniency, but which, in this case, was simply a formality and was never intended to be acted upon. It ended with the words:

> Therefore We do strike you again with excommunication, and declare that like a rotten branch you must be severed from the body lest you infect it. We turn you over to the secular arm. We reject you. We cut you off. We abandon you, begging the same secular arm to mitigate the execution of its sentence upon you with respect to death and the mutilation of your body, and if true signs of penitence appear in you, let the sacrament of penitence be administered to you.

Joan was then handed over to the secular arm, whose duty it was to deliver the final sentence, but as Laurent Guesdon, the deputy of the Bailiff of Rouen, testified, 'Before any civil sentence had been pronounced by either the Bailiff or myself, the executioner took her and dragged her to where the fire was already prepared.'

Manchon, however, in his testimony stated that, without any consultation or sentence, the Bailiff simply waved his hand and said, 'Take her away! Take her away!' Whichever is the true version—and, of course, the testimonies were given many years after the event, when time may have clouded the memories of the witnesses—it is apparent that total confusion reigned at this point, with Joan being committed to the stake with indecent haste.

Joan was to suffer a particularly cruel and agonizing death. Although it was the usual custom for the executioner to lessen the victim's agony by placing green wood close to the feet, which meant that death occurred by suffocation before the flames could take hold, in this case, because of the exceptional height of the platform he would be unable to climb up in order to shorten Joan's suffering.

Of the events which followed, Massieu's testimony is the most complete. As Joan was about to be bound to the stake

> she uttered pious and devout lamentations, and called on the blessed Trinity, and on the blessed and glorious Virgin Mary, and on all the blessed Saints in Paradise, naming many of them in her devotions, her lamentations and her true confession of faith. Also she most humbly begged all manner of people, of whatever condition or rank they might be, and whether of her party or of the other, for their pardon, and asked them kindly to pray for her, at the same time pardoning them any harm they had done her. This she continued to

do for a very long time, perhaps for half an hour, and until the end
... and she asked most fervently to be given a cross, and when an
English soldier who was present heard this he made her a little one
out of wood from the end of a stick and handed it to her. She
received it and kissed it most devoutly, uttering pious lamentations
and acknowledging God our Redeemer, who suffered for our
redemption on the Cross, of which she had there the symbol and
representation. Then she put that cross on her breast between her
body and her clothes, and humbly asked me to let her have the
Crucifix from the church so that she could gaze on it continuously
until her death. And I saw to it that it was brought to her from the
parish church of Saint-Sauveur and she embraced it closely and
long, and clung to it until she was tied to the stake. While she was
praying and piously lamenting I was hard-pressed by the English to
leave her in their hands the sooner to put her to death, saying to me,
as I was doing my best to comfort her, 'Well, priest, will you keep us
here until dinnertime?'

Joan was then bound to the stake, and her cap replaced with a paper mitre bearing the words 'Heretic, Relapse, Apostate, Idolater', at which point a witness said that the English began to laugh. Isambart de la Pierre, who had been sent to bring the processional crucifix from Saint-Sauveur, held it before her 'in order that she might continue to see her Saviour upon the Cross until she died'.

The fire was lit, and as the flames and smoke rose, Joan was heard to invoke the names of St Michael and the saints Catherine and Margaret. She was also heard to cry out, 'Rouen, Rouen, is it here that I must die?', and, 'Oh, Rouen, I fear that you will suffer for my death!' Isambart, still holding the crucifix close to Joan, was told by her to move away from the flames, but to hold the crucifix raised high, so that she could still see it. As he testified: 'In the flames she never ceased until the end to proclaim the holy name of Jesus, and to constantly invoke the saints in Paradise, and in finally giving up her spirit she let her head fall and uttered the name of Jesus for the last time.'

As the flames intensified, and as Joan repeatedly cried out the name of Jesus, Maugier Leparmentier, who had been in charge when she had been threatened with the torture, said that 'even with her last breath she called so loudly on Jesus that all those present could hear her, and almost everyone wept with pity'.

As Joan's loud cries were heard, unrest began to arise among the crowds witnessing the dreadful scene. In the words of one of those present, there was 'murmuring that a great wrong and injustice had been done to Joan'. Another said, 'The majority of those present—there were perhaps ten thousand of them—wept and lamented and said that it was most pitiful...'

It was reported that some of the Church dignitaries fled the scene, unable to bear the sight, together with officials of the Rouen civil authority. Witnesses also recalled the tears of the Bishop of Thérouanne, Louis de Luxembourg, the brother of Jean de Luxembourg, who had sold Joan to the English. The Canon of Rouen, Jean Alespée, 'wept abundantly', and was heard to say, 'I wish that my soul were where I believe the soul of that woman to be.' Jean Tressart, secretary to the King of England, 'wept lamentably over what he had seen', and said, 'We are all lost; we have burnt a holy woman.'

Reaction to Joan's death by Cauchon, the Vice-Inquisitor and other major figures in the trial is not recorded...

The trial notary, the worthy Guillaume Manchon, who had frequently clashed with Cauchon by refusing to enter false testimony against Joan, said, 'I never wept as much for anything that befell me, and could not finally stop weeping for a whole month afterwards. With a part of the money which I was paid for the case, I bought a little missal, which I still possess, to remind me to pray for her.'

When the flames had died down and it was certain that Joan was dead, the executioner, Geoffroy Thérage, was ordered by the English to rake aside the still-burning wood, in order to show her charred and naked body, so that all could see that the witch had not escaped. The wood was then put back and relit so that her body could finally be reduced to ashes.

In Joan's final moments, strange rumours had begun to spread among the crowds, as testified by Thomas Marie, Prior of the convent of Saint-Michel, near Rouen, who had not taken part in the trial but was present at the scene: 'Many there told me that the name of Jesus had been seen written in the flames of the fire in which she was being burnt.'

In the aftermath of Joan's martyrdom, two events were dramatically recalled, again by Isambart de la Pierre:

> One of the English, a soldier who particularly hated Joan, and had sworn that with his own hand he would carry a faggot to her pyre, in the moment when he was doing so and heard her crying upon the name of Jesus in her last moments, was struck with a stupor or a kind of ecstasy. He was taken to a nearby tavern to be restored to his senses with strong drink. And when he had eaten a meal with a friar of the Dominican order, this Englishman confessed to the friar, who was also an Englishman, that he had committed a grievous sin, and repented what he had done against Joan, whom he considered a saint. For it seemed to this Englishman that at the moment when Joan gave up the ghost, he had seen a white dove come out of the flames and fly away in the direction of France.

An even more astonishing event occurred, as de la Pierre related:

> Immediately after the execution, the executioner came to me and my companion, Martin Ladvenu, struck and moved to a marvellous repentance and contrition, all in despair, fearing never to obtain pardon and indulgence from God for what he had done to that saintly woman; and said and affirmed that despite the oil, the sulphur and the charcoal which he had applied, nevertheless he had not by any means been able to consume nor reduce to ashes the heart nor the entrails, at which was he as greatly astonished as by a manifest miracle. He said to us both that he greatly feared he was damned, for he had burnt a saint.

★ ★ ★

Joan's heart would not burn! As Rudolf Steiner expressly pointed out, her mission was not only imprinted in her soul, but 'in her very heart of hearts'—the exalted source from which divinely inspired forces radiated, preserving from destruction this most spiritual of the organs of the human body.

★ ★ ★

When the executioner reported the remarkable phenomenon of Joan's intact heart to the Earl of Warwick and Cardinal Beaufort, they ordered him to throw the entire remains into the Seine, so that no relics would be left to venerate. Joan's incorruptible heart, together with her ashes and the cinders from the pyre, were then wrapped in a sack and taken by the executioner to the Pont Mathilde and thrown into the great river—an act forever enshrined in the poem by August Cordier, 'De Rouen jusqu'a la mer, toute la Seine est sainte'— 'From Rouen to the sea, all the Seine is holy.'

★ ★ ★

Rudolf Steiner said of Joan's martyrdom:

> Joan of Arc was seized within with the forces of the divine spiritual world. What these forces encountered in the soul were the Luciferic Forces, which were powerful and strong at that time. The Maid, through that which she bore within her, was able to conquer them—she became the conqueror of the Luciferic Forces, as is clearly evident to anyone who has the will to see. Her death occurred because all the Luciferic Forces of her enemies joined together and brought it about.
>
> When the Maid of Orléans left the physical world, her soul on passing through the portal of death, declared its readiness to work on at the further developments of events in the form of existence she would be in after her death: and this she did! What the spiritual forces have to carry out takes place, whatever form outer circumstances may take! The enemies of Joan of Arc could bring about her physical death, they could organize the strongest attack; but they could not prevent the accomplishment of her mission.
>
> At the time when the Spiritual Soul was entering the evolution of mankind on Earth, it was difficult for the Beings of the spiritual world next to this earthly existence to approach mankind. The form assumed by earthly events at that time proves that very peculiar conditions were necessary in order to enable the Spirit to find its way into the physical life of mankind. But it shows another thing as well, and in a way that is often most illuminating. It shows how, at a point when the Powers of the past are still at work and those of the future already beginning their activity, one spiritual influence tried to find its way into the earthly life of mankind in vigorous oppo-

sition to another. In the chaos of the Hundred Years' War, which was due to a certain spiritual current unfavourable to the evolution of mankind, events which would otherwise have brought the Spiritual Soul into humanity more quickly were definitely hindered.

This was a time when the spiritual forces, seeking to evolve man according to the potentialities laid in him from the very beginning by yet loftier Divine-Spiritual Powers, encountered their strong adversaries. These adversaries wish to divert man into channels other than those appointed for him from the beginning. If they were to succeed, man would not be able to apply the forces of his origin to his further evolution. His cosmic childhood would remain unfruitful for him. It would become a dying, withering part within his being. The consequence would be that man could then fall a prey to the Luciferic or Ahrimanic powers and lose his own true and proper development. If the adversaries of mankind had succeeded in their efforts—if they had not only put hindrances in the way, but achieved complete success—the entry of the Spiritual Soul could have been prevented.

And so, the mission and death of Joan of Arc made possible the advent of the Spiritual Soul into human life. She not only awakened the consciousness of the French nation by her mission but, as a result of her martyrdom, a further development in the evolution of the human soul, necessary for the future spiritual growth of man, was brought to birth; and this gradually emerges as the epoch of the Spiritual Soul progresses from its beginnings in the fifteenth century.

This development, which is the highest human quality, and which can be seen in its highest expression in her sacrifice, is that which recognizes its own responsibility to the spiritual worlds and to Christ—when it is realized that no external authority, neither Church nor State, can relieve each man and woman of the responsibility to believe and to act according to individual human conscience. Joan of Arc, as the Christ-filled sibyl, her soul strengthened and inspired by Christ, embodied this quality in its most sublime fulfilment, and expressed it in her words, 'God must first be served.'

And the great sacrifice made by Joan of Arc, to bring to birth in the world this awareness of conscience, is expressed by Rudolf Steiner in *Occult History*—in relation to another personality, though he could equally be referring to Joan—when he says that, such a death

> represented with paradoxical grandeur, a most pregnant symbol ... one of those events that is seemingly only a martyrdom, but is in reality a symbol in which spiritual forces, spiritual intimations are coming to expression.

And in relation to this, he also says:

> Before something can come more generally into human life, it must first have been expressed in a single human personality.

And we have seen that this entails great pain and sacrifice on the part of a human being. In the last days of her life, Joan was told by her Spiritual Counsel that she would be delivered by 'a great victory'—she said she did not know what was meant by this and they did not explain further to her. But, in the event, it proved to be her martyrdom that was to be her 'great victory'—a victory over the dark luciferic forces for the benefit of mankind.

16   Rehabilitation

'I had a daughter...' These opening words were spoken on behalf of an elderly woman, who appeared in the great cathedral of Notre Dame in Paris on the morning of 7 November 1455. Supported by her two sons, she approached the three commissioners appointed by Pope Calixtus III, to present her petition containing a formal request for the nullification of a sentence of heresy pronounced almost a quarter of a century before. The woman was Isabelle Romée, the mother of Joan of Arc.

★   ★   ★

The proceedings known as the Trial of Rehabilitation, which would see the reversal of the sentence of heresy against Joan of Arc, would not begin until many years after her death. The main reasons for the delay were, firstly, the ongoing conflict between France and England, and also the long years of strife between Charles VII and Philippe, Duke of Burgundy, which only began to show some signs of peace when a six-year truce between the two sides was signed in December 1431.

A further reason for the delay concerned the city of Rouen; captured by Henry V in 1418, after a long and merciless siege, it would remain in English hands for many years after Joan's death. A bold attempt to free the city was made in 1432 by a French captain, Guillaume de Ricarville who, with a few hundred mercenaries captured the château of Bouvreuil, the place of Joan's incarceration. But a few days later, after a sustained attack, a strong English force regained the château and seized the mercenaries and their leader, and all were subsequently beheaded in the Vieux Marché on the orders of the Duke of Bedford.

During this period, Charles VII, apathetic as always, was still very much under the influence of his long-time councillor, the corrupt Georges de la Trémoille, who had shown such enmity towards Joan when her influence with Charles threatened to undermine his own. The King was finally roused into action when the Constable of France,

Arthur de Richemont, together with members of the royal family, including Charles' mother-in-law, the indomitable Yolande of Aragon, Queen of Sicily, attempted to assassinate Trémoille. The attempt failed, Trémoille was only wounded, but he was permanently banished from court, and it was from this point that the French began to be more active in their military and diplomatic endeavours. In September 1435, lasting peace was finally attained between France and Burgundy when, despite protests from England, the Treaty of Arras was signed. In the same month the Duke of Bedford died in the château of Rouen.

There were many uprisings against English occupation during the early 1430s. In Normandy, Dieppe was restored to France, together with other towns in the area. After two years of misery and near starvation in Paris, due to famine in the countryside, there was an insurrection by the people, following which Constable de Richemont was able to enter and occupy the city with the help of the insurgents on 13 April 1436. Many high-ranking supporters of the English were forced to flee, among them the Bishop of Beauvais, Pierre Cauchon. Joan's prophetic words were now being realized: 'Before seven years have passed, the English will lose a greater gage than they had at Orléans, and they will lose all in France, and this will be accomplished by a great victory that God will send the French.'

The finances of both England and France at this time were in a serious state; the continuous warfare had depleted the coffers of both countries, and although there were some clashes between the two sides there were no major battles. France underwent a series of disasters; the failure of crops, due to bands of mercenaries rampaging through the countryside and terrorizing the farming communities, who were unable to farm their lands, caused deprivation over a wide area. Misery increased in the kingdom when plague broke out, causing the deaths of 50,000 in Paris alone in 1439.

In 1440, Charles, Duke of Orléans, the poet-prince, cousin of Charles VII and half-brother to Dunois, Bastard of Orléans, was finally released from his 25 years of imprisonment in England, his enormous ransom almost paid. He had been captured at Agincourt in 1415, at the age of 24, having been left for dead on the battlefield. Joan had said, 'I know that God greatly loves the Duke of Orléans', and she regarded it as part of her mission to 'cross the sea and return him to France'. At her trial she said, 'I have had more revelations about him than about any man in France, except my King.' In gratitude for Joan's victory at Orléans, he had sent an order from his prison to his treasurer in Orléans to have a robe and tabard made in his livery of vermilion and green, decorated with gold and trimmed with white silk and fur, for Joan to wear at the coronation in Reims.

From 1441, attempts were made by Charles VII's army to recapture various places under English occupation, but with little real success. The discouraged King retired to the Loire to lead a life of indolence and luxury, in which he was eventually joined by his mistress, the 'most beauteous' Agnès Sorel. He lived in this manner for some years, indifferent to the pleas of his advisors to end his extravagant ways, and ignoring all attempts to instil into him the need for further action.

In May 1444, a truce was concluded with England by the marriage of Henry VI to the French princess, Margaret of Anjou. Peace was maintained between the two countries until early in 1449, when the truce was violated by a surprise attack on the château of Fougères, led by a mercenary in the service of England. Reaction to the coup immediately followed, when a now more mature and responsible Charles VII personally led a large army into the area on 17 July, to begin the recovery of Normandy. English forces in the region were weak and towns soon surrendered to the French. Charles established his headquarters in Louviers in August, from where he learned of uprisings against the English in Rouen. He marched towards the city, which quickly fell, and he made his triumphal entry on 10 November. Rouen was restored to France after over 30 years of English occupation.

★ ★ ★

Nineteen years had passed since the trial and death of Joan of Arc—the same number as the years of her life. With Rouen under English rule and with all the eyewitnesses and the trial documents held within the confines of the city, nothing had been known throughout the rest of France during this time of the true circumstances surrounding Joan's fate.

With Rouen now back in French hands, Charles lost no time in setting in motion an inquiry into Joan's trial, and on 15 February 1450 a letter was despatched in his name to his trusted councillor, Guillaume Bouillé, Canon of Noyon Cathedral, authorizing him to initiate the proceedings which would later become known as the Trial of Rehabilitation.

Bouillé's instructions were worded thus:

> Whereas Joan the Maid was taken and apprehended by our ancient enemies and adversaries the English, and brought to this town of Rouen, against whom they caused to be brought proceedings by certain persons ... in which proceedings they did and committed many faults and abuses, to such point that, by means of that trial and the great hatred which our enemies had against her, they iniquitously, cruelly and in defiance of all justice put her to death; therefore we would know the truth of the said trial proceedings and the manner according to which it was carried out. We authorize, command and expressly enjoin that you enquire into and inform yourself diligently on that which is said about it; and ... bring it close and sealed before us and the people of our council...

Bouillé went to work immediately, and on 4 March in Rouen produced his first witness, the notary Guillaume Manchon, who had been present throughout the entire trial. Manchon had signed and sealed every page of his notes and preserved them in the original French, and his evidence lasted a whole day. On the following day, six more witnesses appeared, amongst whom were Isambart de la Pierre, Martin Ladvenu and the usher, Jean Massieu, who gave their firsthand testimony about the trial and Joan's last hours. Also present was Jean Beaupère, one of the leading assessors and a staunch supporter of Cauchon, who had closely questioned Joan during the trial. It was to him that she had given her magnificent reply regarding her state of grace; nevertheless, he could not resist adding to his testimony the sly remark that 'she was very subtle, with a woman's subtlety'.

Upon receiving Bouillé's report, it was immediately obvious to the King that the testimony of these first few witnesses was sufficient to show that the trial had been conducted entirely as a political affair. By succeeding in convicting Joan of heresy the English had been able to discredit her mission and, by so doing, also challenge the right of

Charles to the throne. But his authority alone was not enough to rescind the sentence against Joan. She had been found guilty by the Inquisition and only the Church could reverse that decision. For the moment no further progress was possible and, in fact, six more years were to pass between the Royal Inquiry and the final stages of the Rehabilitation process.

★ ★ ★

Meanwhile, events in France saw the fulfilment of Joan's prophetic words, as the whole of northern France began to fall to the French. Henry VI, whose finances were at a low ebb, pledged the crown jewels in order to raise a large army in a last desperate bid to stop the French advance. Landing at Cherbourg on 15 March 1450, his army, under the command of Thomas Kyriel, marched to Formigny where it was to await reinforcements from the Earl of Somerset's forces stationed in Caen. But before this could happen, the Constable of France and his army arrived unexpectedly and, on 15 April, at the famous battle of Formigny, won a victory which has been called another Agincourt, but this time in reverse. With this final English defeat, the rest of Normandy quickly fell and all the northern territories were soon back in French hands.

★ ★ ★

On 13 August 1451, Pope Nicolas V sent his legate, Guillaume d'Estouteville, to France with the aim of uniting various Christian countries for a possible Crusade against the Turks who, at that time, were threatening Constantinople. D'Estouteville was French and a dedicated patriot, and he was also a second cousin of King Charles. His many tasks must have kept him busy, as it was not until February 1452 that he visited Charles at Tours to discuss the matter of Joan's trial. From there he travelled to Rouen to familiarize himself with the results of Bouillé's inquiry. His next move was to contact the recently appointed Inquisitor-General of France, Jean Bréhal, who from this point would take charge of the proceedings.

This meeting resulted in the opening of the first ecclesiastical inquiry, the findings of which were combined with those of the Royal Inquiry and incorporated into a file to be used for the official

Rehabilitation proceedings. The records of the Trial of Condemnation were studied and other officials were called in to draw up a form of interrogation to be used when examining witnesses. On 2 May, Manchon and others were questioned again, a procedure which led to an even more detailed questionnaire being drawn up, which consisted of 27 very detailed Articles to be used as a basis for the proceedings. These questioned all the flaws and errors in the Trial of Condemnation and were also intended to investigate Joan's character, the causes of her relapse, and her attitude in the last moments of her life.

On 8 May, more witnesses appeared, as well as some of the assessors who had conducted the trial and who, although obviously reluctant to attend, had been summoned and were closely interrogated. Others, who had played no part in the trial but had been witnesses to the events 21 years earlier, willingly gave their testimonies. Missing, were the major figures in Joan's trial: Cauchon had died suddenly in 1442 while being bled by his barber-surgeon; Nicolas Loiseleur, who had posed as Joan's fellow-countryman in the hope of obtaining incriminating evidence against her, had died suddenly in Basle; the promoter of the trial, the vile Jean d'Estivet, had been found drowned in a sewer; Nicolas Midi, who had preached the last interminable sermon to Joan in the Vieux Marché, had died of leprosy some time after the trial. The Vice-Inquisitor, Jean Lemaître, had mysteriously disappeared. Perhaps it was fortunate for them that they did not live to face their own trials of condemnation.

On 22 May, d'Estouteville notified the King that the inquiry was finished, and at the beginning of July visited him at his château at Mehun-sur-Yevre to give him the results of the ecclesiastical inquiry. From this time a new phase in the Rehabilitation process began. With a view to gaining the opinions of various authorities specializing in canon law, Jean Bréhal composed a résumé, known as the *Summarium*, outlining all the charges brought against Joan at the trial on which detailed clarification was requested. Relating to each charge was the question: Would you have reached the same conclusion as the Rouen judges? The importance of this procedure is shown by the fact that many canons and theologians of high repute, both in France and abroad, were consulted.

A lengthy period now followed, when little progress appears to have been made towards the Rehabilitation process, although it can be assumed that the learned doctors were still engaged in studying the lengthy work submitted to them by Bréhal.

★ ★ ★

Throughout this time there was a great deal of political and military activity in Europe and beyond. In France, Charles VII's armies were successful in retaking the last bastions of English rule in Guyenne and Gascony, effectively bringing to an end the Hundred Years' War. Because of the situation in the East, the politically involved Pope Nicolas V—whose permission had to be sought for the Trial of Rehabilitation to begin—was still engaged in urging the Christian countries to a Crusade, but to no avail, and Constantinople fell to the Turks in May 1453.

★ ★ ★

It has been suggested that the minds and energies of those connected with the Rehabilitation process were diverted from taking further action by these more important events. Whatever the case, it was not until 1454, when Guillaume d'Estouteville had been installed as Archbishop of Rouen, that the process began to move forward once again. A decision was taken by one of the doctors consulted in the matter of Joan's case that, as the nearest relatives of the deceased, Isabelle d'Arc and her family should act as plaintiffs in the petition to be presented to the Holy Father. In the middle of the year, Jean Bréhal visited Pope Nicolas in Rome to deliver their request to gain his authorization for the Trial of Rehabilitation to begin.

As the Pope's verdict was awaited, legal counsel were chosen to represent the d'Arc family, headed by Pierre Maugier, a doctor in canon law, together with a number of attorneys whose tasks would be to gather testimony from witnesses in various locations throughout France.

It is not clear as to what stage had been reached in the proceedings when, early in 1455, Pope Nicolas died and was succeeded by Calixtus III. However, the new Pope lost no time in giving his authorization to the appeal and issued his decree on 11 July for the case of Joan's rehabilitation to begin. He commissioned three important churchmen to take charge of the proceedings: Jean Jouvenel des Ursins, Archbishop of Reims, Guillaume Chartier, Bishop of Paris, and Richard Olivier, Bishop of Coutances.

Joan's father and his eldest son, Jacques, had both died—it is not known when or under what circumstances. But after her husband's death Isabelle was invited to live in Orléans in 1440 (possibly by the newly returned Duke Charles), where she lived for the rest of her life on a pension granted by the grateful burghers of the city. Her two surviving sons, Pierre and Jean, now ennobled with the title of *du Lys*, had both received honours and entitlements from the King; Duke Charles would later grant Pierre the hereditary title of the Ile-aux-Boeufs, near Orléans, 'in favour and contemplation of his sister, Joan the Maid'.

In the magnificent setting of the cathedral of Notre Dame in Paris, on the morning of 7 November 1455, the truth about the life of the peasant girl from Domremy was about to unfold. Isabelle and her two sons entered the nave of the cathedral, accompanied by a group of priests and townspeople from Orléans, who had escorted them on their journey to Paris. Awaiting them were the three papal commissioners and the Inquisitor-General, Jean Bréhal. As Isabelle moved forward to present her petition, a large crowd, drawn by the announcement of the ceremony, had been waiting outside, and now surged into the cathedral and began to gather around in ever-increasing numbers, intent on witnessing the dramatic ceremony about to begin.

It is on record that Isabelle, overcome by emotion, knelt before the commissioners with 'pitiable plaints and mournful supplications' during the reading of her moving and poignant plea:

> I had a daughter born in lawful wedlock, whom I had diligently taught the sacraments of baptism and confirmation and had reared in the fear of God and respect for the tradition of the Church, as far as her age and the simplicity of her condition allowed … that having grown up amid fields and pastures she was much in the church and received every month, after due confession, the sacrament of the Eucharist, despite her young age, and gave herself to

fasts and prayers with great devotion and fervour, for the needs of that time were so great which the people suffered and with which she sympathized with all her heart ... yet certain enemies ... in a trial perfidious, violent and iniquitous ... did condemn her ... and put her to death very cruelly by fire ... for the damnation of their souls and in notorious, infamous and irreparable damage done to me, Isabelle, and mine ...

As the words echoed around the nave, they were sympathetically taken up and voiced by the enormous crowd, causing such disorder that the commissioners and Isabelle and her party were obliged to take refuge in the sacristy until order could be restored.

After the ceremony Isabelle was consoled by the priests, and she also received the assurance of the commissioners that everything would now be done to hasten the process to establish Joan's innocence.

On 17 November, Isabelle and her sons appeared before an imposing tribunal in the audience chamber of the Bishop of Paris. All those in high office associated with Joan's case were present for this first session, together with the family's advocate, Pierre Maugier, who would now be able to proceed with his instructions to the attorneys who were to journey to all parts of the realm and begin their interrogations of the witnesses to Joan's life.

The court next moved on to Rouen, where all those involved were required to appear between 12 and 20 December. Public notices were posted and town criers issued proclamations. On 12 December, Guillaume Manchon handed over all the trial documents in his possession and was also examined during the whole of the day on 17 December. A Promoter, Simon Chapitault, had been appointed and questioned again all those who had appeared at the preliminary inquiry. After hearing testimony from Manchon to the effect that the Articles of Accusation had never been read to Joan and how the *cédule* of abjuration had been substituted for another, Chapitault declared that he had sufficient evidence to pronounce the entire trial proceedings to be faulty and corrupt.

Sessions took place in Domremy on 28 January 1456, when all those who had known Joan in childhood were summoned to attend the village church to testify before appointed church dignitaries from

Vaucouleurs and Toul. Simon Chapitault had arrived from Paris in order to investigate the 1431 inquiry which Cauchon had suppressed, because all the evidence was favourable to Joan.

One by one the villagers came forward to give their testimony. The first to appear was one of a number of Joan's godparents, Jean Moreau (now aged about 70), who stated, as many others would do, the good character of Joan's parents and Joan's piety from an early age: 'She went gladly and often to church.' He spoke of the Ladies' or Fairies' Tree and of the superstitions surrounding it, adding that since the Gospel of St John had been read there 'they say the fairies did not come any more'. Of the flight to Neufchâteau, where all the villagers had taken refuge after the attack on Domremy, and about which attempts had been made at the trial to accuse Joan of immoral behaviour, he said she was always to be found in the company of her parents 'because of the soldiers'.

The widow Béatrice d'Estellin (80) spoke of Joan's chaste and well-behaved demeanour—'she went often to church and confessed gladly'—and of her industrious nature both in the home and in the fields. Of the 1431 inquiry, which she remembered taking place, she knew nothing, 'for nobody asked me anything'. Other godmothers testified similarly, as did several more women of the village.

A local priest, Henri Arnoul (64), said Joan used to confess to him 'gladly and often', and the Vicar of Domremy, Jean Colin (60), stated that he had heard her confessions at Vaucouleurs, and 'when she made up her mind to go to France, I saw her mount her horse and ride away . . .' The bell-ringer of Domremy, Perrin Drappier (60), spoke of the times when Joan would scold him for forgetting to ring the church bells for the services.

Next came Joan's childhood friends. Colin (50), used to chide her for being so pious, and Simonin Musnier (44), was nursed by her when he was ill. Hauviette (45), Joan's dearest friend, 'loved her dearly' and 'cried very bitterly about her going', and Mengette (46), Joan's other friend said, 'When she went away she said goodbye to me and prayed God to bless me.' Michel Lebuin (44) and Gérardin d'Epinal (60) to whom she had hinted about her great secret, spoke about this, and also of the times they visited the Ladies' Tree with Joan and the other village children.

Testimony was also given by witnesses to the 1431 inquiry; some involved in gathering evidence spoke of their anger when they were accused by Cauchon's agents of falsifying their information about Joan's character.

A lengthy statement was given by Joan's 'uncle', Durand Laxart, who had so reluctantly agreed to take her to Governor Baudricourt at Vaucouleurs. He gave a detailed account of the events which took place there and, with justifiable pride, ended his testimony, 'I saw her at Reims, at the King's coronation.'

In Vaucouleurs, on 11 February, Jean de Metz (57) and Bertrand de Poulengy (63), Joan's original champions, appeared before the tribunal. Both had been knighted for their services in war 'and for other circumstances', the latter obviously referring to their vital role in the early stages of Joan's mission. Each gave a lengthy account of meeting Joan at Vaucouleurs and of the eleven-day journey on the road to Chinon.

The testimony of Robert de Baudricourt would undoubtedly have been of exceptional interest, but the bluff Governor was by this time dead. Some members of his garrison testified to events at Vaucouleurs at the time. One, Albert d'Ourches (60), a knight who had fought in some of Joan's battles, said he saw her confess to Brother Richard at Senlis and thought she was 'a perfect Christian'.

Henri Le Royer (64) and his wife Catherine (54), in whose home Joan had stayed for the three weeks prior to her departure for Chinon, spoke of the excitement generated in the town by Joan's appearance and the subsequent events. Catherine also recalled her utter astonishment at Joan's statement that she was the virgin who was to restore France.

Later in February, further sessions resumed in Rouen and two further inquiries were ordered to take place. The first was in Orléans, where testimonies were taken from the many ordinary citizens who had known Joan; all were in accord in expressing their admiration and great affection for her, and still loud in their praises for her heroic actions in liberating the city.

The second inquiry took place in Paris where, on 12 May, two important depositions were taken. The first was from Jean, Bastard of Orléans, Comte de Dunois (51), the most faithful of Joan's captains, whose belief in her had never wavered; he had even led an abortive campaign in the Rouen area in an attempt to free her. The next deposition was from Jean, duc d'Alençon (50), Joan's *beau duc*, who was likewise her devoted supporter and friend. Each lengthy testimony bears witness to the great camaraderie which existed between Joan and her two closest companions in arms.

Other depositions were taken from Joan's page, Louis de Coutes, and from her confessor, Jean Pasquerel. Joan's squire, Jean d'Aulon, now knighted and Seneschal of Beaucaire, sent his deposition in writing; he had been appointed to her household from the time of her appearance at Poitiers and was captured with her at Compiègne. His deposition, dated 20 May 1456, was the last of the enormous number which were taken during the entire Rehabilitation proceedings.

On 30 May, a new hearing was opened in Rouen for the sole purpose of allowing any persons who might wish to speak against Rehabilitation to do so; no one came forward. On 2 June, the court declared all the evidence gathered in the course of the inquiry to be officially accepted.

Finally, on 10 June in Paris, the Inquisitor, Jean Bréhal, having received all the documents in the case, drew up a summary known as the *Recollectio*, in which all the charges against Joan at the Trial of Condemnation were compared with her answers, together with all the material obtained in connection with the new trial. During the month, the commissioners made a thorough study of the *Recollectio*, and notices were again posted on all the church doors in Rouen, inviting objectors to come forward; again, none did.

On 2 July, the Promoter, Simon Chapitault, and Guillaume Prevosteau, representing the family, appeared to ask the judges to pronounce Joan's rehabilitation in the name of the Holy See. On 7 July, a meeting took place in the great hall of the episcopal palace in Rouen, where the three pontifical commissioners, the Archbishop of Reims, the Bishop of Paris, the Bishop to Coutances, together with the Inquisitor Jean Bréhal, Simon Chapitault and others, prepared to take part in the final ceremony to proclaim Joan's rehabilitation. Jean d'Arc was present, with his advocates Pierre Maugier and Guillaume Prevosteau. Also present was Martin Ladvenu, but Isambart de la Pierre had meanwhile died.

After the opening ceremonies, the Archbishop of Reims, as President of the court, read aloud the following:

> In consideration of the request of the d'Arc family against the Bishop of Beauvais, the promoter of criminal proceedings and the inquisitor of Rouen ... We, having God only before our eyes, say, pronounce, decree and declare that the said trial and sentence being tainted with fraud, calumny, iniquity, contradiction and manifest errors of fact and of law, including the abjuration and execution ... to be null, invalid, worthless, without effect and annihilated ... We break and annul them and declare that they must be destroyed ... We proclaim that Joan did not contract any taint of infamy and that she shall be and is washed clean of such and, if need be, we wash her clean of such absolutely ...

One of the original copies of the Articles of Accusation was then symbolically torn up, and the court and the entire assembly moved to the cemetery of Saint-Ouen, where the verdict was read again. On the following day, in the Vieux Marché, the verdict was repeated, followed by a solemn service and the erection of a cross on the site of Joan's martyrdom 'to her perpetual memory and that prayers be offered up for the salvation of her soul and those other departed souls'. Orders were also given for crosses to be erected 'both in this city of Rouen and in various other places in the kingdom'. Most of these would survive until the French Revolution, when some would be destroyed by anti-Royalist fervour, but survivors still stand today, along with the enormous number of statuary and other tributes raised to Joan's memory down the centuries.

The final act was undertaken by the man who had devoted five years of his life to Joan's cause, the Inquisitor, Jean Bréhal. He now set off for Rome, to inform the Pope of the outcome of the case, accompanied by Guillaume Bouillé, Charles VII's councillor, who had been instructed by the King to initiate the Rehabilitation proceedings. First stopping on the way to tell the King about the result of the trial, the two then journeyed on to Orléans where a great celebratory banquet was to be held in July—one of many such celebrations to take place throughout France, as Joan's rehabilitation became widely known.

On 27 July 1456, in the splendid surroundings of the banqueting hall in Orléans, the dignitaries of the city were assembled to honour the memory of their great heroine. The special guest at the banquet was Isabelle d'Arc.

With her daughter's reputation restored, and the many years of suffering over Joan's fate now behind her, the old and frail Isabelle retired to a small village outside Orléans, where she died two years later, on 28 November 1458.

Afterword

Rudolf Steiner has pointed out that the state of affairs during the Middle Ages was such that all organizations, all community life, was 'permeated by the powerful and authoritative universalist Catholic impulse moulded by Rome, which dominated and set its seal upon them'. To the extent that all aspects of human life were subordinate to the Roman Catholic impulse, so also national identity suffered the same fate.

Then, at the beginning of the Consciousness Soul age, the idea of nationality began to emerge, especially in France and in England, and we have seen that it was due to the mission of Joan of Arc that the separate national identities of these two nations were made possible: men became conscious of themselves in a new way—as members of nations. Joan expressed this in the words 'God has given France to the French, and England to the English'.

Since that time, consciousness has developed further and is still doing so: people have become conscious of themselves as individuals; first there is the concept of individual nations, then of individual people. The cult of personality has grown, with all its attendant difficulties because, as people have developed an individual, separative life, they have done so without spiritual insight, spiritual knowledge of the world. Development has been under the impulses of natural science and, later, technology—materialism—none of which takes into consideration the spiritual nature of man.

This is a second stage, a stage that continues on into our own day. We are not yet a third of the way through the Consciousness Soul age, but the present time seems to be even more enmeshed in its study and pursuit of the purely physical and material aspects of life, although, as we know, these are necessary developments in evolution.

But in our time we have reached a further stage, a stage when it has become possible for man to attain knowledge of the spiritual world and of himself as a spiritually evolving being; he now has the guidance of spiritual science to enable him to understand why no external authority can relieve him of responsibility as to his beliefs and actions.

And from all these developments since the Middle Ages we see that this possibility began to arise when we come to the nineteenth century—the time when the great battle for man was taking place between Michael and Lucifer and Ahriman—when, in particular, the ahrimanic powers would throw their whole forces into the world.

It is at this time that the life and deeds of Joan of Arc appear again before the consciousness of man, in great clarity and in great detail—this, however, is only the outward sign. In the spiritual world, Michael and all his helpers were preparing for an intense renewal of activity, for when Michael would take on his role as Time Spirit. The other Archangels had, through the ages, exercised their respective roles as the leading Spirits, and now a time was approaching of the greatest significance for man's further spiritual development.

Rudolf Steiner contrasts the time of Joan of Arc with our times in this way:

> The Christ Impulse worked through His Michael Spirit, accomplishing a great task in the fifteenth century for the help and progress of humanity, and there we look into the time when it was necessary that the divine spiritual forces should seek an entrance, through the finest, the gentlest and most subtle, the purest intimacies of the human soul.
>
> That, however, was the last period in which such a thing had to happen. Today it is no longer possible for the divine spiritual forces to descend into the human soul in such an intimate way.
>
> It is still the case in our age that all that orders and rules the great connections is from the spiritual worlds, and we must become conscious of the fact that the forces and impulses that bring things to pass come from the spiritual worlds. In this respect the same holds good today, as at the time of the Maid of Orléans. But the times are different. And what took place at that time in a particular way must be accomplished in a different way in our age and in the time to come. For our age has become quite changed since then; humanity is guided in quite a different way than the age that called forth the impulse from which the Maid of Orléans had to work.
>
> In the future the Christ Impulse must unite with souls in such a way that there shall be human beings in Central Europe who, in

their waking consciousness, by an effort of their conscious spiritual forces in the physical and etheric bodies, shall also unite their ego and their astral body with the Christ Impulse.

In these words by Rudolf Steiner, we recognize another servant of Michael, whose mission at another crucial stage in world evolution was to speak from his great insight of the situation existing today, and of how man may do what is necessary to go forward into the future.

Not since Joan of Arc has anyone spoken out so clearly to the world about Michael and his task for humanity—but today it is not in commands, as it was then. For the times are indeed different—Michael was not the leading Spirit in the fifteenth century, and it was not then possible to work on the human reason and understanding as it is today, when guidance comes in the spiritual science brought to us by Rudolf Steiner.

Both Rudolf Steiner and Joan of Arc were born for necessary and vital deeds in the world. In the lifetime of Joan of Arc she spoke from the depths of her soul, inspiring those around her to accomplish the physical deeds necessary for her time. And today, knowledge and understanding of her final deed—her martyrdom—can become a living inspiration in human hearts.

Today also, Rudolf Steiner speaks to us of the deeds necessary for our time—the deeds of our thoughts, which we can transform when, as he tells us:

> Just as a nature such as that of Joan of Arc had actively to confront the Luciferic forces, so must man today offer resistance to the forces of Ahriman . . . must make himself strong against them . . . as is right, in the Age of Michael.

Principal Sources

Foreword
Rudolf Steiner	*Occult History*, lecture II
Rudolf Steiner	*Christ and the Spiritual World*, lecture 6
Rudolf Steiner	'Thoughts for the Times', lecture 5
Rudolf Steiner	*Karmic Relationships, Vol. III*, lecture VII
Rudolf Steiner	*Christ in Relation to Lucifer and Ahriman*
Emil Bock	*The Three Years*

Introduction
William Shakespeare	*Henry VI, Part 1*
Friedrich Schiller	*The Maid of Orleans*
Robert Southey	*Joan of Arc*
J.E.J. Quicherat (ed.)	*Procès de Condamnation et de réhabilitation de Jeanne d'Arc*
Rudolf Steiner	'Thoughts for the Times', lecture 5

Chapter 1: Domremy
Régine Pernoud	*Joan of Arc*
Rudolf Steiner	*Occult History*, lecture III

Chapter 2: Vaucouleurs
Régine Pernoud	*Joan of Arc*
Régine Pernoud	*The Retrial of Joan of Arc*
Rudolf Steiner	*Christ and the Spiritual World*, lectures 4 & 6

Chapter 3: Chinon
Rudolf Steiner	'Thoughts for the Times', lecture 5
Régine Pernoud	*Joan of Arc*
W.S. Scott	*Jeanne d'Arc*
Bernard Shaw	*Saint Joan*

Chapter 4: Orléans
Rudolf Steiner	*Christ in Relation to Lucifer and Ahriman*
W.S. Scott	*Jeanne d'Arc*
Régine Pernoud	*The Retrial of Joan of Arc*
Régine Pernoud	*Joan of Arc*
Ingvald Raknem	*Joan of Arc*

Chapter 5: The Loire Campaign
Régine Pernoud   *The Retrial of Joan of Arc*
Régine Pernoud   *Joan of Arc*
Rudolf Steiner   *Anthroposophical Ethics*, lecture I

Chapter 6: Reims
Régine Pernoud   *Joan of Arc*

Chapter 7: Towards Paris
Rudolf Steiner   *Harmony of the Creative Word*, lectures 5 & 6

Chapter 8: Victory—and Defeat
Régine Pernoud   *The Retrial of Joan of Arc*
Rudolf Steiner   'Thoughts for the Times', lecture 5

Chapter 9: Capture
Georges Chastellain   In: Quicherat, *Procès*, Vol. 5

Chapter 10: The Final Journey
W.S. Scott   *Jeanne d'Arc*

Chapter 11: Imprisonment
Régine Pernoud   *Joan of Arc*
Rudolf Steiner   'Thoughts for the Times', lecture 5
John Macdonell   *Historical Trials*

Chapter 12: The Trial—Part 1
John Macdonell   *Historical Trials*
Régine Pernoud   *Joan of Arc*
T. Douglas Murray   *Jeanne d'Arc*
W.S. Scott   *The Trial of Joan of Arc*
T. Douglas Murray   *Jeanne d'Arc*
Régine Pernoud   *Joan of Arc*

Chapter 13: The Trial—Part 2
Régine Pernoud   *Joan of Arc*
Régine Pernoud   *The Retrial of Joan of Arc*
T. Douglas Murray   *Jeanne d'Arc*

Chapter 14: Abjuration and Relapse
W.S. Scott   *Jeanne d'Arc*
Régine Pernoud   *The Retrial of Joan of Arc*

Chapter 15: Martyrdom

Régine Pernoud	*The Retrial of Joan of Arc*
W.S. Scott	*Jeanne d'Arc*
Régine Pernoud	*The Retrial of Joan of Arc*
Régine Pernoud	*Joan of Arc*
Rudolf Steiner	'Thoughts for the Times', lecture 5
Rudolf Steiner	*Occult History*, lecture I

Chapter 16: Rehabilitation

Régine Pernoud	*Joan of Arc*
Régine Pernoud	*The Retrial of Joan of Arc*

Afterword

Rudolf Steiner	'Thoughts for the Times', lecture 5

Bibliography

W.P. Barrett, *The Trial of Jeanne d'Arc. A complete translation of the original documents*, with an introduction by W.P. Barrett. George Routledge & Sons, Ltd., London, 1931.

Emil Bock, *The Three Years. The Life of Christ between Baptism and Ascension*. Floris Books, Edinburgh, 1995.

Georges Chastellain, Flemish chronicler and historian 1415–75. In: Quicherat, *Procès de condamnation et de réhabilitation de Jeanne d'Arc*, Vol. 5. Renouard, Paris, 1841–9.

Sir John Macdonell, K.C.B., *Historical Trials. A Selection*. Watts & Co., London, 1931.

T. Douglas Murray, *Jeanne d'Arc. Maid of Orleans, Deliverer of France. Being the Story of her Life, her Achievements, and her Death, as attested on Oath and Set forth in the Original Documents*. Edited by T. Douglas Murray. William Heinemann, London, 1902.

Régine Pernoud, *Joan of Arc. By Herself and Her Witnesses*. Macdonald & Co., London, 1964.

Régine Pernoud, *The Retrial of Joan of Arc. The Evidence at the Trial for Her Rehabilitation*. Methuen & Co., London, 1955.

J.E.J. Quicherat (ed.), *Procès de condamnation et de réhabilitation de Jeanne d'Arc*. 5 vols. Renouard, Paris, 1841–9.

Ingvald Raknem, *Joan of Arc in History, Legend and Literature*. Universitetsforlaget, Oslo, 1971.

Friedrich Schiller, *The Maid of Orleans*. Translated, with an Introduction, Appendix and Notes, by Major-General P. Maxwell. Walter Scott, Ltd., London. (no date).

W.S. Scott, *Jeanne d'Arc. Her Life, Her Death and the Myth*. George G. Harrap & Co., London, 1974.

W.S. Scott, *The Trial of Joan of Arc. Being the verbatim report of the proceedings from the Orleans Manuscript*, translated with an Introduction and Notes by W.S. Scott. The Folio Society, London, 1956.

William Shakespeare, *Henry VI. Part 1*. Edited by Charles Jasper Sisson. Odhams Press, London, 1953.

Bernard Shaw, *Saint Joan. A Chronicle Play in Six Scenes and an Epilogue*. Constable and Company, London, 1924.

Robert Southey, *Joan of Arc. Ballads, Lyrics and Minor Poems*. George Routledge & Co., London, 1857.

Rudolf Steiner, *Anthroposophical Ethics. With an Account of Francis of Assisi.* Three lectures, Norrköping, Sweden, 28 to 30 May 1912. Anthroposophical Publishing Company, London, and Anthroposophic Press, New York, 1928.

Rudolf Steiner, *Christ and the Spiritual World. The Search for the Holy Grail.* Six lectures, Leipzig, 28 December 1913 to 2 January 1914. Rudolf Steiner Press, London, 1963. GA149.

Rudolf Steiner, *Christ in Relation to Lucifer and Ahriman.* One lecture, Linz, 18 May 1915. Anthroposophic Press, New York, 1978. GA159.

Rudolf Steiner, *Harmony of the Creative Word. The Human Being and the Elemental, Animal, Plant and Mineral Kingdoms.* Twelve lectures, Dornach, between 19 October and 11 November 1923. Rudolf Steiner Press, London, 2001. GA230.

Rudolf Steiner, *Karmic Relationships. Esoteric Studies.* Vol. III. Eleven lectures, Dornach, between 1 July and 8 August 1924. Rudolf Steiner Press, London, 1977. GA237.

Rudolf Steiner, *Occult History. Historical Personalities and Events in the Light of Spiritual Science.* Six lectures, Stuttgart, 27 December 1910 to 1 January 1911. Anthroposophical Publishing Company, London, 1957. GA126.

Rudolf Steiner, 'Thoughts for the Times'. Typescript lectures, Series 39. Twelve lectures, Berlin, 1 September 1914 to 5 July 1915, specifically Lecture 5. Formerly held at Rudolf Steiner House Library, London. Purportedly originally published by Marie Steiner in the lectures entitled *Zeitbetrachtungen*.

Additional Sources

Kelly DeVries, *Joan of Arc. A Military Leader.* Sutton Publishing Ltd., Stroud, Gloucestershire, 2003.

Andrew Lang, *The Maid of France. Being the Story of the Life and Death of Jeanne d'Arc.* Longmans, Green and Co., London, 1908.

Régine Pernoud & Marie Véronique Clin, *Joan of Arc. Her Story.* Translated and Revised by Jeremy du Quesnay Adams. St Martin's Press, New York, 1998.

V. Sackville-West, *Saint Joan of Arc.* Doubleday, Doran & Company Inc., New York, 1936.

Rudolf Steiner, *Anthroposophical Leading Thoughts. Anthroposophy as a Path of Knowledge. The Michael Mystery. Leading Thoughts.* Second Study: How the Michael Forces work in the earliest Unfolding of the Spiritual Soul. 7.XII.24. Rudolf Steiner Press, London, 1973. GA26.

A note from the publisher

For more than a quarter of a century, **Temple Lodge Publishing** has made available new thought, ideas and research in the field of spiritual science.

Anthroposophy, as founded by Rudolf Steiner (1861-1925), is commonly known today through its practical applications, principally in education (Steiner-Waldorf schools) and agriculture (biodynamic food and wine). But behind this outer activity stands the core discipline of spiritual science, which continues to be developed and updated. True science can never be static and anthroposophy is living knowledge.

Our list features some of the best contemporary spiritual-scientific work available today, as well as introductory titles. So, visit us online at **www.templelodge.com** and join our emailing list for news on new titles.

If you feel like supporting our work, you can do so by buying our books or making a direct donation (we are a non-profit/charitable organisation).

office@templelodge.com

For the finest books of Science and Spirit